WILMA ELLERSIEK

GIVING LOVE — BRINGING JOY

Hand Gesture Games and Lullabies
in the Mood of the Fifth
for Children Between Birth and Nine

TRANSLATED AND EDITED BY
LYN AND KUNDRY WILLWERTH

WALDORF EARLY CHILDHOOD ASSOCIATION OF NORTH AMERICA

Acknowledgments

This publication was made possible by a grant from the Waldorf Curriculum Fund.

Selection, preparation and translation of the original German texts, songs and games were made possible by a grant from the Future Values Fund of the Anthroposophical Society.

The first editions of the original German texts were published under the titles, *Wiege- und Ruhelieder in der Quintenstimmung and Beruehrungs- und Handgestenspiele* by Wilma Ellersiek, Verlag Freies Geistesleben & Urachhaus, Stuttgart. copyright © Verlag Freies Geistesleben & Urachhaus, GmbH, Stuttgart, Germany, 2001.

This English edition contains material from both original German volumes, selected, edited and translated by Kundry and Lyn Willwerth.

Published by
The Waldorf Early Childhood Association of North America (WECAN)
285 Hungry Hollow Road, Spring Valley, New York 10977 USA.

ISBN: 978-0-9796232-6-4

10 9 8 7 6 5 4 3 2

Illustration and cover: Friedericke Lögters
Musical notations: Ingrid Weidenfeld
Design and typeset: Roland Willwerth
Printed by: AlphaGraphics, 814 Penn Avenue Pittsburgh, PA 15222

Printed in the United States of America

TABLE OF CONTENTS

The child lives even more in his origin.
He struggles into day-consciousness
but his day-consciousness is continually
permeated by night-sleep, by the holy
immersion into the realm of the angels.
When we see children sleeping, we
always have the angelic picture of
the human archetype before us.
Children are able to sleep so whole-heartedly
because they still "know"
this angel aspect of the world.

Kurt von Wistinghausen

Word of Greeting

For some decades I have been deeply engaged with the work of Wilma Ellersiek. She has sown a seed that in my view holds great promise for the future of our children. The materialistic posture of life today, as well as today's state of consciousness and social conditions, give rise to many a traumatic insult to our children's very being.

Out of deep understanding of the young child's soul, Wilma Ellersiek has brought to bear a counterweight to this through her touch and hand-gesture games. Areas open up where a child can live and regain health, while parents and all those responsible for the nurture and education of children are given tools to carry out their tasks with due respect for the child's dignity.

I am deeply thankful for the part I've been able to play in helping this impulse to grow, and to see the fruits it is bearing over the whole earth.

The present edition of this work, which has waited so long for publication, brings me great joy, and I hope for its widespread acceptance and use.

Klara Hattermann, 2001
Co-founder, International Waldorf
Kindergarten Association

Translators' Preface

When I took a class on hand gesture games from Klara Hattermann in 1991 I did not expect to become so intensively involved with the work of Wilma Ellersiek. I knew immediately, however, that these hand gesture games were particularly suited to, and needed by, our children in North America, and for this reason I wanted to translate them into English.

The joy with which the children in my kindergarten entered into the games confirmed this first impression; and I was able, over the years, to play many of these games with them.

I was particularly fortunate that Wilma Ellersiek herself reviewed and participated actively in the translation of the first 25 games.

My aim to transform simple German children's verses into equally simple children's verses in English, yet considering rhyme, meter and vowel colors was greatly aided by my husband Lyn.

Our hope has been to achieve in these games a genuine sound of the English language. We present them here with the hope that they bring you and your children much joy.

This volume of hand gesture games by Wilma Ellersiek consists of selections of material from the German volumes I and II. These volumes, "Lullabies and Rest Songs in the Mood of the Fifth" and "Touching and Hand Gesture Games," contain those songs and games particularly created for the mother-to-be, infant and toddler. More lullabies will be included in volumes III "Spring and Summer" and IV "Fall and Winter," or later volumes.

The size constraint of this first book - ca. 100 pages - also made it necessary to reduce the pedagogical considerations preceding the actual games. All explanations pertaining to the use, execution and musical presentation of the touch games and lullabies have been retained.

Many minds and hands have helped in readying this first volume of Wilma Ellersiek's hand gesture games for publication. We thank our son Roland Willwerth for the layout and overall appearance of this book. Verlag Freies Geistesleben, the

German publisher, generously shared the images from the German edition with us. Ingrid Weidenfeld and Irmela and Jürgen Möller made the manuscripts available for translation. Anne Plaine and Andrea Sutherland helped with proof-reading. Through Joan Almon, The Waldorf Early Childhood Association (WECAN) offered to be the publisher. A generous grant from the Future Values Fund of the Anthroposophical Society made it possible to begin this project. We are also grateful to those colleagues who suggested changes in certain difficult passages in the text and so helped to polish the final product. Our gratitude goes to those mentioned above, and in addition to all those whose goodwill and encouragement have helped bring this book into being.

March 2002
Kundry and Lyn Willwerth

A Word from the Publisher of the English Edition

The Waldorf Early Childhood Association of North America is pleased to publish this collection of games and lullabies developed by Wilma Ellersiek. These games have been shared widely in the Waldorf early childhood movement, first by Klara Hatterman, and later by a devoted circle of individuals including Kundry Willwerth, a longtime Waldorf kindergarten teacher from Ithaca, New York.

For many years, Kundry has worked intensively with Wilma Ellersiek and the international working group to learn the games and share them with others, first in the original German and now also in English, thanks to Kundry's valiant and intensive efforts. The translation of such texts, artistically formed in the German language to evoke very particular qualities and often accompanied by melodies designed to accompany the flow and color of the original language, is no small feat.

We would like to recognize Kundry Willwerth for the great gift, offered through love and joy, that she now shares with educators, parents and children in North America and in the English-speaking world.

December 2002
Susan Howard

Foreword to the German Edition

We owe the touch games or "caresses" presented here to Prof. Wilma Ellersiek. She was asked again and again to publish the games as a book, after presenting them throughout nearly twenty years to smaller or larger groups of people, to mothers and fathers who were interested in the games and learned them. Many individual copies had been handed out in connection with courses and workshops, with handwritten directions and specific instructions and drawings for the games, enabling further practical application and correction. Over the course of years, the author was able to make more or less extensive changes in the games' actual use.

Publication in book format has advantages such as polished presentation and completeness, but also it has drawbacks. Until now Prof. Ellersiek's handwritten descriptions have been distributed at introductory and practical workshops, where participants received handouts of the games presented. Practicing initially under guidance is, even after publication of the books, a desirable way for the games to achieve their optimum effect.

Undisturbed rehearsal in privacy is still needed, just as it was before publication. The contents need to be rehearsed as thoroughly as the playing of a sonata by a musician. There is no use in letting the books stand on the shelf, not working with the games; or, lacking guidance, interpreting the games too subjectively.

How the Games Came into Being

From 1950 to 1981, the author was Professor at the Academy for Music and Theater in Stuttgart, Germany. Her specialties were education in acting, speaking and Dalcroze eurhythmics, as well as staging performances. Together with her colleagues, she has trained entire generations of rhythmists, actors and speech-training specialists.

> "At the peak of her successful career, Wilma Ellersiek turns, with typical whole-hearted decisiveness, to a field of endeavor that promises no spectacular successes: she turns to young children!
>
> Far from all commotion, in the shelter of the Academy, she develops games, texts and songs, and arranges them for mother and child into combinations of 'play-organisms'. The imaginative world of pre-school children, still nourished by creation's archetypes, now becomes her own world. Here she can bring to a common denominator all movements, sounds, hand gestures, articulations of speech that are at her disposal in richest measure… That is not done in a trice, but needs to be prepared as thoroughly as a Bach prelude or a Mozart sonata."[1]

Basic Purpose

From playing with these games, and from communications with the author their motto is clearly: *Giving Love — Bringing Joy.*

It springs from a deeply healing, mercurial impulse, a modern necessity in view of the social distress of our children. This work is indeed mercurial, therapeutic. The author, like many artists, became aware of the need for healing in our time, limiting the scope of her great abilities and placing them in the service of our children. In the years 1967-1968 she began with "rhythmic-musical" games, given to groups of mothers and children in the Academy of Music. The Academy gave her free rein and instituted a new program of study for her activity, as counterpoise to the "early learning programs" then being started. This work took place in concert with Klara Hattermann from the International Waldorf Kindergarten Association. Mrs. Hattermann protected and encouraged the still new and pioneering means of access to the child, for just like anything new and unaccustomed, the touching and hand-gesture games were viewed with suspicion. In 1981-1982 Mrs. Hattermann began to carry the impulse out into the world, finding enthusiastic participants at her seminars, which also fostered the games in far-off lands, through study courses upon their translation into English, Japanese and other languages.

Each era has its own problems. Children are especially vulnerable towards unsure educative practice, technical inundation of the senses, lack of worthy exemplars, lack of movement, and loss or uncertainty of human bonding. Wilma Ellersiek did not limit herself to simply warming over the existing therapeutic arsenal. Her creation was ever new and original, springing from her reading of the needs and character of the children. She also described the method of how to propagate and multiply these creations, always searching, always investigating. Still, she felt her effort to be "inadequate." Herbert Hahn encouraged her with

Rudolf Steiner's remark: "The spirit world accepts enthusiasm as a substitute for perfection."

Inner and Outer Attitude

Although this volume is centered on the first seven years of life, the games can be used, depending on the situation, "for small, big, young, old, healthy, sick, traumatized or special needs children." (Wilma Ellersiek) Intensive work was done, for example, in a curative educational outpatient practice, where their ordering, harmonizing and imitation-inducing effect was experienced. Of special value in this regard were the "touching games," or as Mrs. Ellersiek so nicely puts it, "caresses." Even 6-7 year old rascals can be reached with them (e. g. with "Aye-a - Bye-a - Bocken" or with "Bind-a Bind a Band").

In many children we find a great yearning for objective, loving touch, for bodily awareness and bodily limits which help them to incarnate entirely, right down into their fingertips and toes. Only when a child feels comfortable in his or her body and is well incarnated can healthy contact with the outside world be established. If careful, loving contacts are imprinted in the body, the child can also more easily establish a careful nurturing relation with plants, animals, people and things in their surroundings. The touch games nurture, above all, the sense of contact, the sense of well-being (life) and the sense of the child's own movement. Much that serves later life depends on these senses' wholesome development. From early on, Rudolf Steiner pointed out the importance of care for the senses. The modern science of child development links with the conclusions of spiritual science and recognizes the fundamental importance of these basic senses.

In the first year of life the daily rhythms of care-giving, carried out cheerfully and calmly, lend security and contentment to the child.[2] If, then, one begins later with the games of touch, they need to be done lovingly, cheerfully and gently,

being aware of the small child's needs and patiently entering with senses open to the reaction of the child. In the third year of life a growing openness is noticed, perhaps at first indirectly. For example, the mother at first plays the game upon herself, a sibling or a doll, and then waits until the child would like to do it too. In the case of very sensitive or autistic children one avoids direct contact (often over a long time), making the gestures over or around the child, always with cushioning air space between. In work with school age children up to second or third grade, a separate space is needed to practice the games of touch, one child at a time. Then children who in a group might reject the games as "too babyish" will happily accept them. Through this they undergo a maturing transformation.

Grown-ups also undergo a change when we practice the touch games. We achieve inner peace and concentration when we unite our entire ego-awareness with the movements. When the games are carried out with care, warmth and love stream through our arms and hands. Laying aside our emotions, we feel ourselves placed into a wide expanse binding us to the world from which the child has come to us. Then we may become mediators; a different quality enters our touch and we create a space for the child upon earth in which he or she can grow and prosper.

Dear Reader,

Surely by now you would like to choose some games and begin to practice. But first you find a text placed before you for your attention!

Mrs. Ellersiek expresses her thoughts about the meaning of touch, the inner posture and the formation of speech to be attempted by the practitioner. Reading through these texts only once certainly is not enough. Experience has shown how these texts constantly reveal themselves and are enlivened more and more, attuning us increasingly toward working with them according to the intent of their creator.

In curative educational practice too, as described at the end of the foreword, these texts have been guides, reread and reconsidered again and again; they also have created an inner mood for courses and workshops. From of this strength it has been possible to bring to the children the help that they need today.

February 2001
Dr. Jürgen and Irmela Möller

[1] Karl Lorenz: "Rhythmik in der Erziehung," Heft 3, 1981

[2] See essay by Emmi Pickler: "Friedliche Babys - Zufriedene Mütter" [Peaceful Babies -Happy Mothers] (Herder Verlag), which describes this kind of care-giving, which avoids "institutionalism" in orphanages. The essay offers impressive support for Wilma Ellersiek's principles.

Hand Gesture Games

"Caresses"

"Caresses" are little rhythmic-musical finger, hand and touch games that mother, father, or caregiver can bring to the child. Some are suitable even for a baby only a few weeks old. These little games, used with the "Mood of the Fifth Lullabies," make possible a joyful and above all anxiety-free contact between small child and surrounding world. Thereby these games can help the child significantly upon the arduous path into life on earth.

Children incarnate through bumping up against the physical world. As a complement to this they need to experience tender, gentle caressing touch. Through this they can feel themselves invited to unite in full trust and confidence with the earthly world. Gentle protective gestures develop the faculty of tender, delicate behavior toward things, plants, animals and other humans beings. They create the basis of respect towards life and the readiness to protect and preserve it.

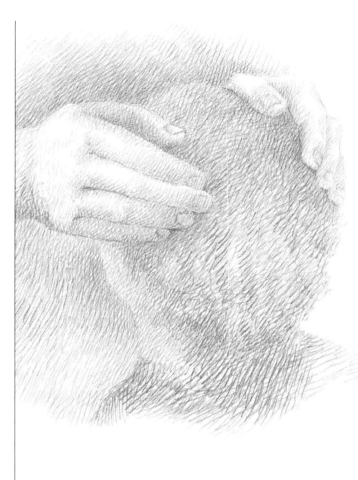

Bodily contact between human beings may convey the expression of very egocentric feelings, such as anger or desire. A touch may also, however, express assurance or the security that we accept the other and recognize his or her right to be. Human beings feel the need for acceptance as individuals by those around them.

From childhood on, individuals differ widely in their readiness to touch others or to be touched by them. Mothers and fathers can cause lasting hurt by avoiding bodily contact with their children. On the other hand, they can heal wounds of shock or serious pain through their touch. Not without reason are rites of "laying on hands" widespread in all societies, conferring blessing, for example, by laying the hand upon the head of another.

Caresses, as they are here meant to be understood, are given by the adult to the child out of a spirit of reverence. The adult turns to the child caringly, protectively, asking nothing for herself.

A certain reserve is necessary to refrain from allowing feelings of egotism or self-gratification to enter.

> "But a caress is abode and shelter.
> I caress the child so as to protect him
> And thereby he receives a sign
> Upon the velvet of his face."
>
> *Antoine de Saint-Exupéry*

Rhythmic-musical caresses and story games need to be carried out in a form that remains free from subjective emotions and opinions. The action of touch is an objective, suprapersonal, pure motion! One needs to orient oneself to the spiritual essence of motion and speech. The pulsating flowing (rhythm), the breathing swinging (sound), the cosmic energies and formative forces working in them constitute the foundation of their formation. Thus the loving, gentle caress of a human being attains a higher quality and more profound effect; it becomes an unselfish, caring gesture that is able to create a protective shelter for the powers of childhood and the essence of the child. Reverent in nature, it takes place on a different level than ordinary contact. Through the artistically formed caresses and story games with their series of syllables and rhymed verses, the necessary objectivity can be achieved. Religious, spirit-endowed contact experience is transmitted, which can call forth the feeling for the Divine.

In the education of the small child, we must become aware that the child lives not only in the earthly surroundings, but also in the larger cosmic, heavenly world. The more such heavenly forces flow in through the selfless touch-gesture, entering and permeating the whole body of the child, the more we can become mediators through our demeanor and suppress our subjective feelings and opinions. Then, through the sense of touch, the child can discover the cosmic order.

At birth a child receives a body not yet fully formed. In the first seven years of life, the child is entirely enmeshed in the creative process of developing organs, forming and re-forming the body. This creative process or "creative wielding" is the work of the angel (form-spirits), consummated in bodily becoming. The child in the first seven years of life is devout, thoroughly devout, in the body. Through the selfless touch of the human hand and voice, the child can feel pure bodily comfort, which the artistically conceived caresses are meant to call forth, unsullied by human egotism, whereas ordinary bodily touch usually tends toward egotistic pleasure. While these experiences remain in the unconscious, the bodily foundation is laid for later mental and spiritual trust in God.

In these short moments of special devotion through touch raised above everyday life, parents and caregivers can become aware, again and again, that in striving for objective, suprapersonal touch gestures, we can in a special way become collaborators in the work of the angels. From this can come the strength needed to become a helper of the the child's angel in the task of education.

Molding of Language for the Games

The manner in which language is used is of great importance for all the rhythmic-musically created caresses and touch games. In these games, the literal meaning retreats into the background; the child should be presented with the rhythmic-musical and dynamic action of the language. The pliability of the sounds, the gesture of the words, the rhythmical pulse beat of the stream of language, the melody of sounds, the variety of "tone hues," the dynamic of the varying strength of tone, are what must engage our attention.

Our speech nearly sings; it is lifted up and away from the prosaic. We must avoid the conventional "sing-song" interval of the third, through which an unintended stereotypic speech melody arises. Instead, the sound is made to correspond with the gesture of speech, whereby a variety of pitch and timbre arises which defies even conventional musical notation. Thus a richly diverse range of pitch and tone, and an objective musicality without dramatization can be experienced.

Thus the creative, artistic spirit of the language, rather than its conceptual aspect, stands in the forefront. By immersing himself in the process of forming sounds as it takes place, and in making the word-gestures together with the adult, the child comes to know and live within the form through which the language arises. This is archetypal gesture (movement) rather than mere abstract concept or descriptive speech image.

In this ongoing process the child can embody the language within himself and thus undergo a profound, comprehensive spiritual shaping. In this formative process both speech and language have a creative function. The child's organism itself is molded and the foundation is built for the creative, imaginative use of language.

The way in which the mother or father speaks with the child always serves as an examples. Every healthy child learns from examples through imitation. In the following essay Klara Hattermann describes wonderfully how the child becomes familiar with the world through imitation.

The Child Becomes Familiar with the World through Imitation[1]

Let us look at the small child from birth through the first years of life in reference to his physical body and his psychological-spiritual faculties. To begin with he enters the world helpless and unsuited for his task on earth. The head, with its fontanelle not yet closed, is large in comparison to the body. The limbs are not perfected, the body not completely formed; even the bodily organs have not yet achieved the form they will retain. The child lies horizontally, the little feet and hands still reaching for heaven, in contrast to an animal, whose limbs are generally oriented toward earth, and soon after birth are supporting the body to walk upon the earth. The kicking and wriggling of the newborn are spontaneous, uncontrolled, uncoordinated, and aimless. Language also needs a long development. Psychological impulses are at first largely bound to the body, while consciousness remains in a state of twilight.

How does the child find his way into the earth world? How does he learn to adapt to this world? Can we as parents or caregivers, for example, teach him to walk or to speak? We become aware of our powerlessness when a child comes to earth and is unable to stand upright and walk or to speak.

Children are living puzzles for us. From an earthbound perspective they seem deficient. On the other hand, every parent who nurtures and protects a child with love and compassion knows the great radiant power coming from that child. He learns to live in the world with wonder, openness and devotion, offering infinite trust to human beings and revealing in his life expressions a powerful will pervading the whole body.

By way of example: Mother steps to the bed of her several month-old baby. She smiles, while her voice reflects joy and happiness for the child given into her care. The child responds with more than a smile; the intimate contact is imparted to the entire body. The limbs take up the cozy feeling and begin to wriggle; the lips articulate sounds. The loving inclination of the mother is shared with the child, who opens up to it. He doesn't understand the conceptual content of the words, but the love and joy immediately awaken the intensity and activity of the will and thus act to fashion organs within the still soft and pliable body. The organs of speech, such as the larynx, begin to mature and the breath becomes deeper.

The Child Needs Security

Security and affection liberate in the child latent powers that sleep in him and want to be wakened. These are soul-spiritual powers pertaining to his individuality. The human being originates in spirit realms (in other words, divine or heavenly regions). From there the child brings with him a power, most intensely active in earliest childhood, when the child still lives in a dreamy state in the world, and diminishing around the eighth year. This power is imitation. It is through this that the foundations of human existence are attained:

- orientation in physical space: walking;
- social concourse from human to human in soul space: speech;
- grasp of elementary concepts in mind or spiritual space: thought.

The child learns these faculties without conscious intellectual instruction; yet without the example of others he would never attain them. Only in relation to these examples can the child's ego-being become oriented and develop.

The child takes an exceptional interest in all movement in his surroundings, especially in the actions of other people. From the general perception of movements and facial expressions he absorbs what is essential and imitates it ingeniously. He lives as a unity with his surroundings. The following observation of a child may serve to clarify what is meant: A furniture mover comes into the room with a heavy chest. The three-year-old boy stands in wonder beside his mother and observes intently how the workman carries the load and places the chest onto the floor. During the next few days, the boy plays only furniture-mover. He gets himself an empty cardboard carton, lifts it on his shoulder and imitates, right into the muscular tension, the gesture of the moving man: the bent back, the heavy tread, the tense facial features, and finally the relaxation of putting down the load. Finally he wipes the sweat from his brow with the back of his hand.

In the child's further development after the third year, new faculties awaken that are revealed as powers of imagination. These come to expression above all in the child's play. They reflect, from within, the child's outer surroundings. Imaginative play is also based on imitation, but actions in the surroundings are not just taken over unchanged. The child becomes creative, slipping into the role of human or animal or imitating technical motions. Objects are adapted and transformed. Imagine, for example, all the things a cloth can become: the cloak of a costume; a sea for ships to traverse; knotted, it becomes one of the best possible dolls. This new connecting with the world creates joy, sympathy for earthly existence, and lust for life. Creative powers are spirit powers actively molding the child. Not yet crippled by intellectual thinking, the flow of the child's actions is influenced directly by these powers. Play, for the child, is sacred earnestness, not conditioned to bring results, as is the work of the adult. The child needs free space to be individually active without distraction within his surroundings and to digest his impressions in a childlike way. One can experience the uniqueness of each child's individuality in the choice of motifs and the intensity of activity.

Why do we find so many three-year-olds with premature health problems, aggressive behavior or disturbed movement, who are anxious and inhibited as they approach the world? Unable to play, such children are spectators, allowing events to pass them by.

Often adults have little real understanding for the small child. Their knowledge and deeds are often imprinted by a materialistic view of the world. Self-comfort, egotism and dissatisfaction are often the result, carried over involuntarily into the nursery with the attitude that the child must be prepared in all possible haste for the harsh realities of the world.

Only in a protective shelter which offers the child security, love and warmth, can the faculty of imitation work in a healthy way. The loss of such protection leads to dwindling of this power and therewith to a crippling of creative activity.

Today there are tendencies at work, unfriendly to childhood, that remove the protection from the children. Play rooms laden with complete technical toys and apparatus do not offer possibilities for developing imaginative play or stimulate creative activity. For this reason, toys should be simple. "Educational" toys, developed through the intellect of the adult, are quite out of place in this early phase of childhood, as they call forth precocious intellectual activity and thus hinder the vital forces of life and growth.

From what is described above we learn that children need to find their direction from the human being. As adults we are called upon to give children worthy examples through our own behavior and inner attitude. Colossal effort is needed in today's world to counter harmful effects with positive influences on children. These include:

- efforts toward self-knowledge and self-discipline;
- respect for the spiritual origin of the human being;
- striving to know the human essence and the laws of development of body, mind and soul.

Artistic activity is also essential. Through such approaches, adults can develop a fresh understanding for lively play and a sense for what is coming into being in the child…[1]

[1] This essay was written by Klara Hattermann, published in "Weleda-Almanach."

Movements

As is clearly indicated in the preceding essay, the small child is always interested in movements in his or her surroundings, and especially in the actions of people. The child gains orientation from examples of movement. Therefore, it becomes all the more important for the adult to develop suitably expressive gestures in working with rhythmic-musical caresses, hand gesture and finger games with regard to the mood they present. Generally the touch games need to be played with warm hands. All movements should be soft and fluid; the younger the child the more tender the touch itself must be. Special care in this regard is also called for in the case of handicapped or sick children. The child's head and upper body are especially sensitive. Children only become accepting of touch in these zones at the age of about 2½ years. Some children will play along earlier; for instance, if the adult plays a game with an elder sibling, the younger child soon puts forth his or her head and wants to be given a "present" too.

When a present is given, i. e. when the adult plays a touch game with the child, the adult should look bright and happy. However, her facial expression is completely secondary. Of primary importance is the movement of the hands. For self-touching games, as well as for all hand gesture and finger games, the gaze of the adult needs to be upon the hands as soon as she prepares to carry out a new gesture. Then turn your gaze to the child. Thus the gaze is constantly shuttling between hands and child or children. Be careful, however, not to incite restlessness. This alternation must be well rehearsed! In order for the movements to form a unity with the speech, the movements need to be prepared before the corresponding words are spoken. The texts and the movements need to be so thoroughly worked out and rehearsed that no thought pauses take place.

In order to have lively, natural gestures for games having to do with animals, flowers or other natural phenomena, it is helpful for us as adults inwardly to visualize the animal, flower, snowflake, etc. Clearly calling to mind all their characteristic features, we then must try to transform their essence through our hands into a fitting gesture. Of the utmost importance is time! Children have all the time in the world, and it is healing for adults to leave plenty of time for playing a game. The effect is greatly enhanced when games and caresses are carried out with as much calmness as possible.

In repeating the games, the adult should touch the various places on the body in the same tempo, to allow the calming effect of touch and a feeling of security to arise. To play touch games longer than ten minutes at a time is inadvisable. It is much better and more effective to play a short game with the child several times during the day, each one for a short time.

Many of the touch-games collected here are archetypes for joyful discovery and exploration of the most significant human organ of knowledge, action and expression: the hand with its fingers. The growth and structuring of the Broca speech center in the brain, so essential for the faculty of active speech, are fostered by touching the child's fingers, especially of the right hand. Beyond that, the caresses are especially well suited as a gentle aid to incarnation. The more cautious the touch, the more effective it is. In the case of very sensitive or autistic children, one may hardly touch at all, or even leave a cushion of air between the body of the child and one's own hand.

The descriptions for carrying out the touches and hand gestures are always addressed to the grown-ups. While in most cases it will be the mother who takes up the games, it would be lovely if the father would also make one or another game "his own." In orphanages, kindergartens, or other care-giving facilities, it is natural for both male and female caregivers to use these games, but also grandparents, godparents and in fact anyone interested may feel spoken to when the inclusive term "grown-up" or "adult" is used.

In the game instructions, the following abbreviations are used to designate the fingers:

T = Thumb
P = Pointer (Index finger)
M = Middle finger
R = Ring finger
Pi = Pinky

The toes are numbered: the big toe is #1, the little toe #5.

The foot-touching games may be played (with warm hands, of course) either with or without socks covering the foot.

The games are in the following order: The very first in the book are for the mother-to-be. They provide impulses for making contact with the yet unborn baby. They also help the mother to achieve a composed, joyful attitude, whereby a happy, health-bringing connection with the baby may be established. Then there are short verses for the prematurely born baby. Following these come hand and foot touch-games that may be played even with very young babies. After these are games which focus on various places on the body such as feet, calves, knees, belly, etc. The latter part of the book encompasses the touch-games for the head and upper body, for which the child is not ready until about 2 ½ years of age. The very last four games concern a special theme; that in which the very small child is held and carried in the arms.

Verses and Games for the Mother-to-be and the Newborn

Bonding between Mother and Child before Birth

Not until the beginning of the 1970's did research begin into the phenomenon of mother and newborn often meeting each other after birth as "old friends," accommodating, seeking, consoling, gazing at each other.[1] Prebirth bonding does not take place automatically, but requires time, love and interest. With these conditions in place, many psychological disturbances that we encounter are compensated for.

It is known that unborn children hear, for example, the mother's heartbeat as well as music and speech in the environment; that they taste, move and rehearse the use of all senses and that they react to the emotions of their mother-to-be.

There are essentially three paths by which bonding contact may be established.

1. Through the umbilical cord. The supply of nutrients is unavoidable. Even a mother who does not emotionally accept her baby remains in biological contact.

2. Through behavior. Both mother and child communicate. When unborn infants feel unwell, are frightened, scared or confused, they kick more violently. This has been verified in hundreds of cases. The mother communicates with her child as well. One of the most typical maternal behaviors is stroking the abdomen. This comforting gesture can be observed among pregnant women the world over, and usually succeeds in calming the unborn child.

3. The third connection may be described as spiritual, containing physiological elements as mediators and expressed through behavior. It is best described as empathy, love, interest and care and effects the unborn infant profoundly and compre-

hensively. The child can feel that it is expected and the mother can become attentive to messages from the child, who in turn asks that she be ready to listen. "The child has lots to say, and deserves to be listened to."[2]

On the part of the mother, we find that calm, happy women with an abundance of love have a greater probability of having alert, enterprising children. On the other hand ambivalence and rejection are hostile to life and frequently give rise to miscarriages. Clearly the child has sensitive "antennae," and notices even a gentle tinge of emotion. Intense and long-lasting anxiety can be harmful. Hormones pouring into the blood through fear or stress represent an attack on the unborn child and endanger the bonding between mother and child.

Obstetricians have often confirmed the fact that the soft voice of the mother can calm a restless baby in her womb. Moreover, unborn children seem to love classical music. It fosters their bodily and mental development within the mother's body. Finally, it has been possible to show that babies, if spoken to often in their embryonic state, later learn to speak more easily. The mother should embrace the child in her belly with her hands; the baby already then cuddles into the hands and receives security.

[1] *Die vorgeburtliche Bindung zwischen Mutter und Kind:* Essay by Dr. Jürgen Möller, Hannover, Germany.
[2] *The Pre-birth Connection Between Mother and Child:* Thomas Verny, M.D. and John Kelly; Delta, 1994.

Kickeree

The mother-to-be speaks:
(melodious, almost singing, calm, with pauses)

WHAT COULD IT BE — YOU KICKEREE,
KICKING WITH YOUR TINY KNEE?
I ASK ME: WHAT,
ARE YOU GLAD OR NOT?
I'LL DO IT OFT;
STROKE–STROKE, WARM AND SOFT –
STROKE–STROKE SOFT.
STROKE–STROKE, WARM AND SOFT –
STROKE–STROKE SOFT.
KICKEREE — QUIET BE!

TEXT:

1 What could it be —
   you kickeree,
2 Kicking with your tiny knee?

3 I ask me: what,
4 Are you glad or not?

5 I'll do it oft:
6 Stroke-stroke,
   L. ⤺ ⤻R.
   warm and soft -
   L. ⤺ ⤻ R.
7 Stroke-stroke soft.

8 Stroke-stroke,
   warm and soft -
9 Stroke-stroke soft.
10 Kickeree — quiet be!

TOUCH:

1 Lay hands on belly.

2 Lift hands, then return
   to belly.
3 Hands remain in place.
4 Lift hands at: "are you glad"
   and lay back at "or not."
5 Hands remain in place.
6 Very gently stroke belly
   from the inner side to the
   outer side.

7 First "stroke": stroke from
   lower belly up to the breasts;
   second "stroke": from previous position stroke down
   on both sides bringing
   hands together on the belly;
   at "soft" leave hands at rest.

8 Repeat as in 6.

9 Repeat as in 7.
10 Hands remain at rest on
   belly; breathe deeply.

Repeat verse if the kicking has
not decreased or has increased.

YOU'RE ON YOUR WAY

(In expectation)

I HEAR YOU SAY:
YOU'RE ON YOUR WAY!

ON YOUR WAY
TO THE EARTH TO ME
MY DEAREST BABY TO BE.

I HEAR YOU SAY:
YOU'RE ON YOUR WAY!

MY HEART IN ME
BEATS JOYFULLY!

MY BABY DEAR
I AWAIT YOU HERE!

TEXT:

TOUCH:

The expectant mother lies on her back on a warm pad. To help relax the legs, place a tubular pillow under the bend of your knee. If necessary, put a flat cushion under your head.

1 I hear you say:

2 You're on your way!

3 Silent movement:

4 On your way to the earth
                          to me

1 Lift arms lightly - palms open to the heavens. If this is too tiring, support upper arms on the floor.

2 Move hands toward your body while lifting arms a bit more.

3 Lift arms (hands) higher so that they open to above like a large bowl.

4 In an arch move hands down to the middle so that the hanging fingertips point to the chest, but don't touch.

It is important to allow yourself time for each movement and touch, listening to what has been said, so that communication between mother and child can happen. Also allow time for deeply relaxed breathing.

24

5	my dearest baby to be.	5	Move hands horizontally (palms down) to abdomen and at: "to be," touch down gently. Let hands rest there a bit.
6	I hear you say:	6	Repeat as in 1.
7	You're on your way!	7	Repeat as in 2.
8	My heart in me beats joyfully!	8	Rest crossed hands on chest (near your heart).
9	My baby dear	9	Move hands horizontally to abdomen without touching. At: "baby," gently rest hands feeling the baby under them.
10	I await you here!	10	Move hands from your body and lay them on the mat, palms open to heaven, in a welcoming gesture.
11	Silent movement	11	Slowly and gently return hands to your abdomen, speaking:
12	--- await you here!	12	Leave hands at rest.

As You Come to Me I'll Love You Fervently

(For the infant with special needs)

I GAZE UPON YOUR BODY SMALL
AND SEE: UPON IT LIES A FLAW.
I LOVE YOU AS YOU COME TO ME
AND I SHALL LOVE YOU FERVENTLY.

AS YOU HAVE COME, MY DEAREST STAR,
I'LL LOVE YOU JUST THE WAY YOU ARE.

I WOULD TEND YOU AND DEFEND YOU;
I WOULD HELP YOU GAIN ON EARTH
YOUR HUMAN WORTH.

DOUBT AND SADNESS WITHIN ME HERE
ARE NO HELP TO YOU, POOR DEAR.
THEY DARE NOT DAUNT ME;
STRENGTH MAY GOD GRANT ME
LIFE'S ROCKY WAY WITH YOU TO PLY,
OUR DESTINY TOGETHER TRY.

THE ANGEL I WOULD PRAY
TO GUIDE US EVER ON OUR WAY.

With My Hands
(For the premature infant)

WITH MY HANDS
I COVER YOU.

WITH MY HANDS
I ENWRAP YOU FINE.

YOU BEST, YOU DEAREST BABY MINE,
WITHIN MY VEIL OF LOVE
YOU MAY CLING,
YOU ARE SAFE THEREIN.

Two possibilities to speak to the baby:

a. Hold hands over the incubator or rest them on the incubator.

b. On the changing table or on your lap lovingly cover the child with your hands.

RHYTHMIC – MUSICAL HAND AND BODY TOUCH GAMES

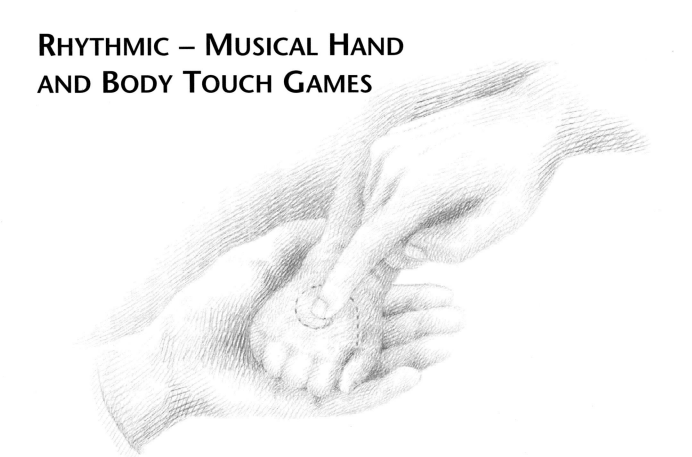

Bind-a Bind a Band

BIND-A BIND A BAND
ALL AROUND YOUR HAND.

RING-A RING-A-LING
ON YOUR FINGERLING.

SO FINE — SO FINE
IS BABY* MINE!

TEXT:

1 Bind-a bind a band

2 All around your hand.
3 Ring-a ring-a-ling

4 On your fingerling.

5 So fine — so fine

TOUCH:

1 Slightly lift the child's arm above the wrist with your left hand and gently circles the child's wrist with the pointer** of your right hand. The slow movement is accompanied with a melodious "sing-song."

2 Repeat movement 1.

3 With thumb and three fingers of the right hand, place the "ring" on the child's right ring fingertip.

4 With gentle twisting motion push "ring" down to the finger root. Slightly lift the voice and in the end at "fingerling" leave the voice floating until it dies down.

5 With the fingertips of your right hand touch the child's wrist gently where the "band" (bracelet) has been put. At the second "so fine," touch the "ring" at the root of the ring finger with your thumb and pointer. Speak slowly and melodiously.

*Here the name of the child may be used.
**See "Movements," page 19

6   Is baby mine!

6   With your right hand, stroke the child's whole hand caressingly, covering the little fist fondly and shaking it lightly at the word "mine." Again hold the voice suspended.

Tip - Tap - Tip - Tap - Tap

TIP - TAP - TIP - TAP - TAP
WHO JUST CAME?
IT IS THE TIPPY -
TAPPYMAN - TAPPYMAN -
TAPPYMAN.
AYE–AYE–!

TEXT:

1   Tip- Tap - Tip - Tap - Tap
    T*   P   M   R   PI

2   Who just came? It
    PI   R   M   P

3   is the Tip - py -
    P M R   PI

4   Tappyman - Tappyman -
                Tappyman.

5   Aye-aye-!

TOUCH:

1   Touch the fingernails of the child's loosely rolled-up right hand very lightly with pointer and middle finger, in sequence.

2   Again with pointer and middle finger, touch the middle joints of the child's fingers in reversed sequence.

3   Now pointer and middle finger touch the child's knuckles.

4   Drum on the top of the child's hand with all fingertips.

5   Cover the child's hand with one or both of yours and squeeze it lovingly.

This touching with the fingertips and the concluding "drumming" can also be used on other parts of the body. One can "tip" from the hand up the lower arm and then let the tappyman dance at the elbow, either inside or outside. The same from elbow to shoulder, or from foot to knee or bend of knee, from knee to belly or from bend of knee to the child's bottom, from belly to under the chin. Discover where the child's favorite place is. At the foot the adult tips, starting at the big toe, in sequence to the small toe, back again to the big toe and again to the small toe. Use the text from 1 to 3. At "Tappyman - Tappyman - Tappyman", drum with the fingertips very gently on top of the foot. At: "Aye-aye-!" enclose foot lovingly with your hands and squeeze gently.

*See "Movements," page 19

31

Snailyman

THE SNAILYMAN CREEPS FROM HIS SHELL.
HE STRETCHES OUT HIS FEELERS WELL.
STUBB! STUBB!
HE PULLS THEM BACK AGAIN
AND CREEPS BACK HOME,
THE SNAILYMAN.

TEXT:

1 The snailyman creeps from his shell

2 He stretches out his feelers well.

3 Stubb! Stubb!

TOUCH:

1 The child's right hand (loose fist) rests on bed, table or left palm of the adult. With your right pointertip,* draw a spiral unwinding to the right on the back of the child's hand (starting in the middle) down to the base of the thumb. Speak melodiously at "snail's pace." Lengthen word syllables.

2 Insert your thumb- and pointertips in the space between the child's thumb and pointer at the base. With the nail side of your fingertips, slide along the inside of the child's fingers and thus stretch the child's thumb and pointer as "feelers." Having arrived at the child's fingertips, hold the "feelers" in their stretched position for a while.

3 Now remove fingers and tap against the "feelers" with your thumb- and pointertips. It should be surprising but not scary. Gentle touch.

It is also possible to draw the snail in the child's palm. Be very gentle, as the center of the hand, the ego-area of the hand, is especially sensitive. Caution is needed for very young or sick children when touching the palm. First start on the back of the hand, later in the palm, or take turns. The adult needs to sense what the children enjoy and what is healing. Role exchange between adult and child is also possible.

*See "Movements," page 19

4	He pulls them back again	4	Gently push child's fingers back into a loose fist.
5	And creeps back home,	5	With right pointertip, starting at thumb base, now begin to draw an involuting spiral (to the left) on the back of the child's hand until you have reached the middle of the hand. Speak at "snail's pace," melodiously. At the end, "back home," tickle hand delicately.
6	The snailyman.	6	Gently cover the child's loose fist with your hands (the snailyman sits safely in his shell). The voice remains floating at the end.

Fat Jack and Thin Lena

FAT JACK AND THIN LENA,
TALL PAUL AND CROOKED LANCE
AND THE LITTLE DOROTHY — THEY ALL DO A DANCE!
DANCING SLOWLY: TRA — LA — LA — LA,
SLOWLY: TRA — LA — LA — LA — LA!
DANCING FASTER, FASTER, FASTER: TRALLALALLLALALLLALA! —
TRALLALALLLALALLLALA! — TRALLALALLLALALLLA! — STOP!
DONE.

TEXT:

1 Fat Jack and thin Lena,
  T*   P
 Tall Paul and
  M
 crooked Lance
   R
 And the little Dorothy —
    PI

2 they all do a dance!
  PI R M P T

3 Dan-cing slow-ly: Tra —
  T P M R PI
 la — la — la, slowly:
  T P M R PI
 tra — la — la — la — la!
  T   P   M R PI

TOUCH:

1 Hold the child's right hand loosely in your left hand. Set the fingertips of your right hand about the child's fingers, one at a time, and delicately stroke up the finger from base to tip, then wiggle the finger a little while naming it.

2 Rhythmically, and one at a time, tip on the child's fingertips, starting with the pinky.

3 The adult's fingers dance around in the child's palm, not in the middle, but around the middle, lightly touching with the fingertips.

The adult must sense if the child would like to repeat the whole game or only the last three "trallalallalas" with the "stop!" and the "done." You can also continue playing with the child's left hand, but end by playing once more with the right hand.

Children familiar with this game will like to play with the adult's hand, particularly the fast dancing.

Word use: "Tip" = light, feathery touch.
*See "Movements," page 19

4 Dan-cing fast-er, fast-er,
   T   P   M R PI T
fast-er:
   P   M
Trallalallalallala! —
Trallalallalallala!
Trallalallalallala! — Stop!

4 The tempo increases, yet each fingertip touches the child's palm in rhythm until the third "faster". Then "drum" freely but in rhythm on the palm around the middle. At "Stop!" clap the child's hand lightly as if to say: "It's enough!" After each "Trallalallalallala" make a small pause.

5 Done.

5 At "Done," to calm the child, lovingly stroke his hand from wrist to finger-tips. Then bend the child's fingers, cover the little fist with your own and squeeze it gently (allow yourself time). This gesture is done silently.

Zoob-a-zoob Zoob

Doob — doob — doob — doob — doob.
Zoob — zoob — zoob-a-zoob zoob.
Aye! — Aye! — Shoom-shey.
Shoom-shey!

TEXT:

1 Doob* — doob —
   PI**   R
   doob — doob — doob.
      M   P   T

2 Zoob — zoob —
      T   P
   zoob-a-zoob zoob.
      M   R   PI

3 Aye! — aye! —

4 Shoom — shey.

5 Shoom — shey!

TOUCH:

1 Hold the child's lower arm at wrist, fingers pointing up. With the tip of your pointer lightly tap on each of the child's fingernails, from pinky to thumb, in sequence.

2 In sequence, from thumb to pinky, pull the child's fingertips very gently.

3 Slide your own palm across the child's palm, from the wrist to the fingertips. Say: "Aye!" very drawn out, almost singing, two times.

4 Slide your hand along the child's hand starting at the wrist, at a slow "shey," causing the child's fingers to roll into a fist. Slide across rolled-in fingers to wrist.

5 Repeat as in 4. At the end, cover the child's fist and squeeze it lovingly and gently. Depending on the hand's size this may be done with only the sliding hand, or both hands, after carefully letting wrist go, so that the child's fist is warmly surrounded.

If the child so desires, this game can be repeated, but not longer then five minutes. You can take turns with the hands, ending with the right hand. The game can also be used as a foot-touching game, transferring the tapping and pulling to the toes. At "Aye," slide your hand along sole of foot from heel to toes, twice. At "shoom-shey," the first time, slide your hand from ankles to toes along instep of foot. At the second "shoom-shey," encircle the foot with your hands and squeeze lovingly.

  *Pronunciation: "oo" as in "cook."
**See "Movements," page 19

Crawly — Crawly — Crawl

CRAWLY — CRAWLY — CRAWL —
WITH LOTS OF LEGS BOTH SHORT AND SMALL
COMES AT A CRAWL A BEETLE SMALL.
CRAWLY — CRAWLY — CRAWL —
BEETLE SMALL — BEETLE SMALL —
CRAWLS INTO ITS LEAFY NEST
AND TAKES A REST! — AND TAKES A REST!

TEXT:

1 Crawly — crawly — crawl —

2 With lots of legs both short and small

3 Comes at a crawl a beetle small.

4 Crawly — crawly — crawl —

5 Beetle small — beetle small —

6 Crawls into its leafy nest

7 And takes a rest! — And takes a rest!

TOUCH:

1 The right hand with all its fingers is the "beetle small." It crawls from the hip onto the right thigh with very swift and light finger movements.

2 Continue crawling in a curve to the middle of the thigh.

3 Continue crawling from the middle of the thigh to the knee and remain there a short while.

4 Return crawling from up the knee to the middle of the thigh in almost a straight line.

5 Continue further back in a curve to thigh.

6 Rest left hand on your left thigh, forming a hollow place for the "leafy nest." With the right hand crawl across from the right thigh underneath the left hand. There the beetle stops.

7 The beetle sits quietly underneath the left hand. Speak very slowly, in a sing-song, letting the sound fade away.

This game can also be played as a "touching game." The hand of the adult as the "beetle small" crawls around on the child's body. The beetle can crawl into its leafy nest under the child's hand, or under his armpit, knee, chin, nape of neck, etc. Roles in this game can also be exchanged.

Naturally the left hand can also take a turn to be the beetle. However, end the game with the right hand. In the end the beetle can be rocked to sleep with a lullaby in the mood of the fifth.

Rain

RAINING DROPS A-RUNNING
ON MY WINDOW DRUMMING:
DOPPA — DOPPA — DOP,
DOPPA — DOPPA — DOP!

DRIPPING RAINDROPS SPRINGING,
YOU CAN HEAR THEM RINGING:
TENG — TENG — TENG,
TENG — TENG — TENG!

DOWN THE PANE THEY HURRY,
DROPS OF RAIN A-FLURRY:
ROLLA — RILLA — ROLL,
ROLLA — RILLA — ROLL!

AND AGAINST THE WINDOW GOES
FLAT, QUITE FLAT, MY BABY'S NOSE.

TEXT:

1   Raining drops a-running
    On my window drumming:

TOUCH:

1   Right hand: fingertips
    as raindrops.
    Left hand: Upright palm
    as "window." From above,
    move right hand with wig-
    gling fingers down to left
    palm. At "drumming," tap
    twice against left palm
    with pointertip.*

This game can also be played
as a partner game. Then the
child's hand is the "window"
and the adult's fingers the
"rain." The adult's nose is
pressed "flat" against the
child's hand. Parts may also
be exchanged.

 *See "Movements," page 19

38

2   Doppa — doppa — dop,
    Doppa — doppa — dop!

3   Dripping raindrops
                springing,
    You can hear them ringing:

4   Teng — teng — teng,
    Teng — teng — teng!

5   Down the pane they hurry,
    Drops of rain a-flurry:

6   Rolla — rilla — roll,
    Rolla — rilla — roll!

7   And against the window
                goes

8   Flat, quite flat, my baby's
                nose.

2   Drum against left palm with all fingertips of your right hand. It is raining.

3   Movements as in 1. At "springing," snap against left palm with thumb and pointer. For the second line repeat movements, but snap against palm at "ringing."

4   For each "teng," snap against palm. You could also alternate thumb and middle finger with pointer and thumb.

5   The fingertips of the right hand slide gently from the fingertips of the left hand along the palm to the wrist, even as far as the elbow, twice.

6   Movements as in 5, but this time in a wavy line. Move same distance as in 5.

7   Move your nose toward your upright left hand and at "flat," touch it against your palm, so that it is possible to speak without difficulty.

8   At "quite flat," press your nose gently against palm. Dissolve gesture, then nod at the child with a smile, perhaps tipping his nose gently with your right pointer.

Wiggle — Waggle

WRIGGLE — WIGGLE — WAGGLE — TOES,

PADDY — PADDY — FOOT THAT GOES,

IN THE SOCK SLIP-SLIPPING DEEP,

SLIP-SLIPPING DEEP.

WARM, MY SWEETIE, WARM MUST KEEP.

WRIGGLE — WIGGLE — WAGGLE — TOES,

PADDY — PADDY — FOOT THAT GOES,

IN THE SOCK SLIP-SLIPPING DEEP,

SLIP-SLIPPING DEEP.

WARM, MY SWEETIE, WARM MUST KEEP.

BOOTS WE PULL ON ANYHOW.

FIRST THIS ONE: PULLA-PULL!

THEN THAT ONE: PULLA-PULL!

TIE A BOW.

FOR OUR WALK YOU'RE READY NOW.

TEXT:	TOUCH:
1 Wrig-gle — wig-gle — 5 4 3 2	1 Gently tip on toes, rhythmically, starting with small toe.*
2 wag-gle — toes, 1 1	2 Tip twice on the big toe. At "toes," touch all toes.
3 <u>Pa</u>ddy — <u>pa</u>ddy — <u>foot</u>	3 Holding sole in one hand, at underlined syllables pat the foot with the other hand.
4 that goes,	4 Holding foot with both hands lift it slightly, then set it down.
5 In the sock	5 Make a "sock" with both hands by joining wrists, edges of thumbs upward.
6 slip-slipping deep,	6 Slip on "sock" from the foot edges up the calf or over the knee, stretching the word "deep" accordingly.

Word use: "Tip" = light, feathery touch.
*See "Movements," page 19

7 Slip-slipping deep.	7 Slip "sock" on again, this time across top of foot and sole, up the calf or over the knee.
8 Warm, my sweetie, warm must keep.	8 Enclose foot with both hands. At second "warm" give a gentle, loving squeeze. For a "knee-sock" gently enclose knee with both hands
9 Wrig-gle -- wig-gle -- 5 4 3 2	9 Repeat for the left foot, from 1 to 8.
10 Boots we pull on anyhow.	10 Show the child the "boots": Hollow hands, palms up, held side by side.
11 First this one:	11 Slightly raise right hand as "boot."
12 Pulla-pull!	12 Pull on "boot": pull right hollow hand, covered by left hand, under and over the foot and at the second "pull" pull the boot over the heel.
13 Then that one:	13 Slightly raise left hand as "boot".
14 Pulla-pull!	14 Pull on the second "boot" in two actions, too, but this time the hollow hand is the left one. Here the tying of the boots may be added.
15 Tie a bow.	15 On each "boot" tie an imaginary bow, first right, then left. For buttons, zippers and other closures change the text, as in "button up" or "zip-a-zip".
16 For our walk you're ready now.	16 Gently grasp each foot with your hands simultaneously, then move the feet in opposite directions up and down and at "ready now" end movement and set feet down.

Doo — Pi — Does

Doo — Pi* — Doo — Pi — Does!**
I tip on your toes.
Doo — Pi — Doo — Pi — Doot!***
I tip on your foot.
Doo — Pi — Doo — Pi — Deel!
I tightly clasp your heel.
Hold firmly in my hand your foot.
Doo — Pi — Doo — Pi — Doot!

TEXT:

1   Doo — pi — doo — pi
     1   2   3   4
                      — does!
                           5
    I tip on your toes.
    1 2 3 4   5

2   Doo — pi — doo — pi
                      — doot!
    I tip on your foot.

3   Doo — pi — doo — pi
                      — deel!

4   I tightly clasp your heel.

5   Hold firmly in my hand
                      your foot.

6   Doo — pi — doo — pi
                      — doot!

TOUCH:

1   The child's feet can be touched one after the other or both feet simultaneously. Starting with the big toe "1" tip lightly on all toes one after the other.

2   Half as fast, tip gently from the toes to the ankle joint along top of foot.

3   Tip around the ankle to the back.

4   Lovingly hold the heel. At "heel" squeeze gently, then hold it a moment silently.

5   Position hand so that it cradles the whole sole and encloses the foot as far as possible. Again hold it a little while silently.

6   At the two syllables "doo" lightly swing the enclosed feet down rhythmically. Pronounce the "doot" slowly. Gently squeeze foot, then put it down and let go.

When touching both feet simultaneously, you can say "deet" and "feet," if you prefer.

Pronunciation note:
  * "pi" as in tip.
  ** Rhymes with toes.
  *** Rhymes with foot.

Word use: "Tip" = light, feathery touch.

Aye-a — Bye-a

AYE-A — BYE-A — BOCKEN
YOU'LL GET A LOVING SNOCKEN.
AYE-A — BYE-A — BOUT,
SNICK — SNOCK — OUT.

TEXT:

1 Silent

2 Aye-a — bye-a —

3 bocken

4 Silent

5 You'll get a loving
6 snocken.

7 Silent
8 Aye-a — bye-a —
9 bout,
10 Snick — snock —

11 out.

GESTURES:

1 With both hands, indicate a small roof above the child's head.

2 While speaking, very gently slide down hands along temples and cheeks until ball of hands touch lower jaw. Do this airily, hardly touching.

3 Press palms lightly against cheeks.

4 Remove hands, look at the child.

5 As you speak, nod and smile.
6 Very gently pluck both cheeks simultaneously.

7 As in 1.
8 As in 2.
9 As in 3.
10 At "snick" very gently pluck at the nose with tips of right thumb and pointer;* at "snock" with both hands very gently pluck both cheeks as in 6.

11 Touch palms to child's cheeks and lightly press. Alternately, while pressing cheeks pull child's head to your shoulder. Another way: Without touching cheeks, hug the child. Speak the word "out" very slowly.

The younger the child, the more sensitive he is to being touched on the head and chest! In these areas, the child is only ready to be touched at about two and a half years of age. Some small children will participate earlier. If, for example, the educator plays this game with older children or parents, the little child may also present his head and get a "present". Soon he will want to do the touching with mother.

After about age two and one half the child will distribute the "present" with joy and perseverance to all around her.

This game is the archetypal picture of tenderness! The game is introduced with the words: "I'll give you a present."

*See "Movements," page 19

Ma - Ma - Moh

MA-MA-MOH, MA-MA-MOH, GREAT, BIG TOE!

MA-MA-MOH, MA-MA- MOH, LITTLE TOE!

MA-MA- MEE, MA-MA-MEE, ROLY* KNEE!

MA-MA-MUMMY, MA-MA-MUMMY, YOUR ROUND TUMMY!

MA-MA-MOH, MA-MA-MOH, LOVE YOU SO!

MA-MA-MOH, MA-MA-MOH, LOVE YOU SOOOO!

TEXT:

1 Ma-ma-moh, ma-ma-moh,
     5   4   3   2

2 great, big toe!

3 Ma-ma-moh, ma-ma-moh,
     1   2   3   4

4 little toe!

5 Ma-ma-mee, ma-ma-mee,

6 roly knee!

7 Ma-ma-mummy,
         ma-ma-mummy!

8 your round tummy!

9 Ma-ma-moh, ma-ma-moh,

TOUCH:

1 On underlined syllables the adult tips gently on child's toes with her fingertips. Start with small toe** (5). Continue in speech rhythm toward big toe.

2 With thumb, pointer and middle fingertips rub big toe lovingly.

3 As in 1, but start with big toe.

4 As in 2, rub little toe.

5 On underlined syllables the adult tips gently along top of foot up the leg to the knee.

6 Slowly speak the word "roly" while moving fingertips around knee. At the word "knee" cover it with your hand and pat it repeatedly.

7 Tip across thigh further up to tummy.

8 At the words "your round" stroke over child's tummy, at "tummy" rest hands on it, then pat repeatedly.

9 Tip on hands in given rhythm.

Child's position: If the child lies down or sits, then touch both sides with your hands simultaneously. If the child lies in your arms touch one side with one hand.

  *Pronunciation note: roly as in roly-poly.

**See "Movements," page 19
Word use: "Tip" = light,
        feathery touch.

10 love you so!	10 Completely cover child's hands with one of yours. At the word "so" shake it gently.	With very sensitive children or autistic children, delete steps 12 and 13; repeat 10 instead.
11 <u>Ma</u>-ma-<u>moh</u>, <u>ma</u>-ma-<u>moh</u>,	11 As in 9.	
12 love you	12 Open wide both your arms and smile at child.	
13 soooooo!	13 Embrace child while rocking a bit to and fro.	

Bzzzzzzz

"Jest"

Bzzzzzzzzz!

Zzzzz

Zzzzzzzzz

Zzzzz

Zzt!

Tickle - tickle - tickle - tickle!

Bzzzzzzzz!

Zzzzz

Zzzzzzzzz

Zzzzz

Zzt!

Tickle - tickle - tickle - tickle!

Bzzzz - zzzz - zzt!

TEXT:	MOVEMENTS:
1 Bzzzzzzzz!	1 Stick pointer* out of your loosely rolled right hand as a "fly." Thumb lies lightly on loosely rolled fingers. The "fly" appears from behind your the back, flying up to about neck height.

2 Zzzzz	2 Down and forward in an arc.
3 Zzzzzzzzz	3 Down and left to middle.
4 Zzzzz	4 Up and in a loop.
5 Zzt!	5 Straight to the back of the child's left hand.
6 Tickle - tickle - tickle - tickle	6 With your right pointertip tickle hand lightly and delicately (fly legs). May be repeated.

Hum the "bzzzz" and "zzzz" with deep voice, swelling and decreasing. Speak the "tickle - tickle - tickle - tickle" with a high, soft voice at constant pitch:

It is important that the "fly" lands on and tickles the adult first. This helps the children to conquer their shyness and makes them wish for a visit by the "fly."

In the beginning let the "fly" come only once or at most twice to land and tickle. The child will then ask for a repeat. Later the child can show where he wants the "fly" to go, even away from his body. After a while he will let the "fly" fly, land and tickle himself with much joy and decide where it lands: by himself, by other people or objects. Go along with the child's suggestions. This

46

7 a Bzzzzzzz!

   b Zzzz
   c Zzzzzzz

   d Zzzzz

   e Zzt!

8 Tickle - tickle - tickle -
                    tickle
9 Bzzzzzzzzz (to: Zzt!)

10 Tickle - tickle - tickle -
                    tickle!
11 Bzzzzzzzz (to: Zzt!)

12 Tickle - tickle - tickle -
                    tickle!
13 Bzzzzzzzzz (to: Zzt!)

7 a "Fly" flies away from
      hand in an arc from
      under to right
      (stomach height),
   b an arc to the left,
   c an arc from under to the
      right (neck height),
   d in a loop from above to
      the right,
   e and lands on the
      right cheek.
8 Tickle cheek with "fly
   legs." May be repeated.
9 Again "fly" flies to the
   child in 4 arcs and lands
   with Zzt! on his hand.
10 Tickle the hand with
   "fly legs."
11 "Fly" flies in 4 arcs (as in 7
   a-e) and lands on the
   child's cheek.
12 Tickle cheek with
   "fly legs."
13 "Fly" flies back to right
   shoulder in four arcs and
   disappears in a loop up
   and behind back. Smile at
   the child.

play is an archetypal picture of
encounter in jest.

   *See "Movements," page 19

47

Visitor

FLI-FLAH-FLUTTER — FLUTTER-BY -
BUTTERFLY CALLS ON MY CHILD.
SITS DOWN ON HER HEAD,
ON BOTH EYES AND ON HER NOSE,
THEN ON HER CHEEKS, BOTH RIGHT AND LEFT,
AND DOWN UPON HER CHIN.
AT LAST SHE GETS A KISS!

THEN BUTTERFLY FLUTTERS AWAY:
FLI-FLAH-FLUTTER-FLARI-EYE —
FLI-FLAH-FLUTTER-FLY —
GOOD-BYE, MY CHILD, GOOD-BYE! —

TEXT:

MOVEMENTS:

*See "Movements," page 19

1 Fli-flah-flutter — flutter-by-
Butterfly calls on my child.

1 The adult's right hand is the
butterfly. All fingers and
thumb are tightly joined and
together are moved as "wing"
from the finger roots. Wrist
and fingers stay quiet.
Fly-path:
"Fli-fla-flutter"
fly in an arc to the right,
outward.
"Flutter-by."
Fly in an arc to the left,
inward.
"Butterfly calls on my child"

Fly right, in an arc, outward
and up above the child's head.

2 Sits down on her head,

2 The pointertip* is now the
butterfly. The pointer pro-
trudes from the lightly
rolled fist. Touch the mentioned body parts lightly
with the pointertip.

3 On both eyes	3 Touch the right eye above the closed eyelid underneath the eyebrow with right pointertip at "both" and touch the left eye in the same way at "eyes."
4 and on her nose,	4 Sit a moment on the tip of the nose, wiggling the fingertip lightly. Speak slowly: "nose."
5 Then on her cheeks, both right and left,	5 The pointer "flies" up in an arc, first to the right, then to the left cheek, each time touching lightly.
6 And down upon her chin.	6 As with the nose sit a moment and tickle lightly. After the tickling, sit quiet a moment.
7 At last she gets a kiss!	7 At "last," move finger and set it as "kiss" on the middle of the upper lip, pressing lightly.
8 Then butterfly flutters away:	8 Remove your hand from the child in an arc upward, forming again the "wing" gesture. In the given rhythm do the flutter movement.

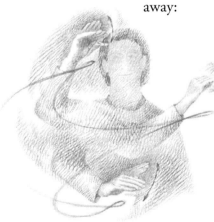

9 Fli-flah-flutter-flari-eye —	9 Continue fluttering in given rhythm, arcs further and further to the right, outward.
10 Fli-flah-flutter-fly — Good-bye, my child, good-bye! —	10 Fly arcs still further to the right until at the final "good-bye" the butterfly flies off straight to the right.

Burra-fuzz

<u>NOTATION:</u> ● ≈ ONE PULSATION (BASIC UNIT) | ⊘ ≈ ●● | ◯ ≈ ●●●● |
●⊘ ≈ ●●● | ⌣ ≈ EXTEND NOTE LENGTH (FERMATA) | ∿ ≈ VOICE VIBRATION
VERY FAST, AS WHEN LAUGHING | ●̇ ≈ STACCATO | ⌒ ≈ ONE BREATH

TEXT:

TOUCH:

*See "Movements," page 19

1   Buzzzzzz (silent)

2   Buzz-buzz-buzz,

3   buzz-buzz-buzz,

4   the little beetle Burrafuzz

5   He buzzes through the air,
    he does, buzz-buzz-buzz.

6   And now he buzzes, com-
    ing close, and lands on lit-
    tle Annie's nose!

7   He tickles our baby so, a-
    tickle, tickle with his toe.

8   Hey!

9   What is this, this tickle?

10 My baby has to

---

1   The right, relaxed fist
    (thumb rests on middle
    finger) lies on your right
    thigh with the pointer,*
    slightly bent, sticking out.
    The pointertip is the bee-
    tle. At "buzzzzzz" it flies
    up in an arc toward the
    left and then completes a
    circle back to its starting
    point, without voice
    accompaniment, in one
    continuous movement

2   and then swings to the right.

3   Then the little beetle swings
    to the left, a little higher

4   again to the right, a little
    higher yet

5   and again to the left,
    even higher. Then repeat 2
    and 3 for "buzz-etc."

6   Now follow the shown
    fly path landing on the
    child's nose.

7   With your pointertip tickle
    the tip of the child's nose.

8   In a small arc the beetle flies
    from the tip to the base of the
    nose. At "Hey," make your
    voice vibrate.

9   With fingertip, very lightly
    tickle the base of the child's
    nose, barely touching.

10 In a small arc the beetle flies
    back to the nose tip, sitting
    down at "giggle."

51

11 gi-gi-gi-gi-gi-gle.

11 Because the child giggles the beetle does not succeed in landing on the nose tip. Tap at the nose three times with your pointertip and flie off again in a little arc.

12 Hachoo!

12 The beetle lands and tickles. Then through the sneezing it is flung up at "choo!"

13 Then tumbles Burrafuzz three times through the air, he does,

13 The beetle flies the shown path.

14 And flies away with buzz-buzz-buzz, buzz-buzz-buzz, buzz-buzz-buzz!

14 Starting at the word, "fly," move off in a straight line upward and out to the right.

15 Bye-bye! My little Burra-fuzz! Bye-bye! — Bye-bye!

15 When your hand has moved to the end of your reach change from "flying" to waving.

Ba - Ba - Bor

BA-BA-BOR! — *SHUT THE DOOR!*

BA-BA-BOUT! — *PEEP OUT!*

BA-BA-BOR! — *SHUT THE DOOR!*

BA-BA-BOUT! — *PEEP OUT!*

BA-BA-BOR! — *SHUT THE DOOR!*

BA-BA-BAA! — *THERE YOU ARE!*

THERE YOU ARE, MY CHILD, THERE YOU ARE!

TEXT:

TOUCH:

A   The player makes the movements to another

B   The player makes the movements to himself

With a small child the adult should do the gestures to herself until the child wishes to be touched.

The game of disappearing -

1 Ba-ba-bor!

2 Shut the door!

3 Ba-ba-bout!

4 Peep out!
5 Ba-ba-bor!
6 Shut the door!
7 Ba-ba-bout
8 Peep out!
9 Ba-ba-bor! — Shut the door!
10 Ba-ba-baa!

11 There you are!

12 There you are, my child,

13 there you are!

1 Move hands together from the side toward the middle until the face is covered. The face should be barely touched, only slightly on the forehead with fingertips. If the game is played on the child, the edges of the pinkies* touch the child's cheeks. If you play on yourself, the thumb edges touch your cheeks. Keep fingers loose, so that some light can shine through. Speak the sound "bor" slowly, stretching "boh-h-hr."

2 Hold hands quietly across face. Stretch the "oo" in door to "doh-h-hr."

3 Carefully open hands like shutters at a window. The pinky edge (thumb edge) continues to touch the cheek.

4 Nod and smile at the child.
5 Same as 1.
6 Same as 2.
7 Same as 3.
8 Same as 4.
9 Same as 1 and 2.
10 Open hands wide enough that they stand to either side of the head, palms toward audience.

11 In this "openness" nod to the child happily. Pronounce "ah-h-re" long.

12 Lay hands together before breastbone. Hold there.

13 If you touch yourself, smilingly nod to the child, tap on his nose or hug him. If you touch the child, only smile and nod.

reappearing is played by most children at a certain age. Even when mother (or the child himself) only covers the eyes with her hand, the child is effectively "gone."

It would be wrong if the adult would correct the child: "but you are not gone." The adult must play along. He must affirm the child's intent of "not wanting to be there." Anything else would be a mis-understanding of the situation. To be able to disappear and reappear is part of a healthy development in the child's life experience. It is the founda-tion of consciousness of free-dom in later life.

*See "Movements," page 19

Soft as Down

SOFT AS DOWN
ON YOUR CROWN.
SOFT AS DOWN
ON YOUR CROWN.
CRAWLY — CRAWLY — CRAWLY — CRIP.
ZIP — ZIP!
CRAWLY — CRAWLY — CRAWLY — CRIP.
ZIP — ZIP!

TEXT:	HAND MOVEMENTS:	*See "Movements," page 19
1　Soft as down on your crown.	1　With the fingertips of both hands stroke very gently from the hairline (forehead) through the child's hair to the crown of the head bearly touching the child's skin. All fingers wiggle lightly.	
2　Soft as down on your crown.	2　Same gentle movement as in 1, from the head's crown to the hairline in the nape of the neck.	
3　Crawly — crawly — crawly — crip.	3　Light tickling with fingertips in the nape of the neck up to the ears.	
4　Zip — zip!	4　With the tips of thumbs and pointers* pull lightly, simultaneously on both ear lobes.	
5　Crawly — crawly — crawly — crip.	5　With fingertips, tickle neck under chin.	
6　Zip — zip!　Further play variations:	6　as in 4.	
7　Crawly — crawly — crawly — crip.	7　Light tickling with fingertips from the ears down to the shoulders.	
8　Zip — zip!	8　as in 4, but pull at shoulders.	
9　Crawly — crawly — crawly — crip.	9　Light tickling with fingertips from shoulders to elbows.	
10　Zip — zip!	10　As in 4, but pull elbows.	

54

11 Crawly — crawly —
       crawly — crip.

11 Tickle down from elbows to the hands (fingers).

12 Zip — zip!

12 As in 4, but pull on fingers.

13 Crawly — crawly —
       crawly — crip.

13 Turn child around so that mother is behind child; or mother steps behind child. Lightly tickle with fingertips from the back of the head to the nape of the neck.

14 Zip — zip!

14 As in 4, but pull at neck.

15 Crawly — crawly —
       crawly — crip.

15 Lightly tickle with fingertips from neck to shoulder blades.

16 Zip — zip!

16 As in 4, but pull at shoulder blades.

17 Crawly — crawly —
       crawly — crip.

17 Lightly tickle with fingertips from shoulder blades down to child's bottom.

18 Zip — zip!

18 As in 4, but pull lightly at bottom. Then lay your hands, fingertips pointing down, for a moment on the child's bottom.

19 Aye!

19 With flat hands, fingertips up, move down back from neck to bottom, very cautiously. Do everything in a calming way, speaking in a sing-song. All finger touches must be very gentle as if a layer of air is between you and the child's body.

Drop — Drop — Droppeli

Drop — drop — droppeli
on your toppeli!
Drop — drop — droppeli
on your nose!
Drop — drop — droppeli
on your toes!
Drop — drop — droppeli
wet all goes! —

TEXT:

1   Drop — drop — droppeli
    on your toppeli!

2   Silent movement

3   Drop — drop — droppeli
4   on your nose

5   Silent movement
6   Drop — drop — droppeli
7   on your toes!

8   Silent movement
9   Drop — drop — droppeli
10 Wet — wet —
            wet all goes! —

GESTURES:

1   Lift arms high above head, elbows not completely stretched through. Palms face in the direction to the audience and are slightly tilted down. While fingers are constantly moving (fingertips are the "rain drops") move hands down to head and at the word "toppeli" touch head gently with fingertips.

2   Lift hands slowly to same position as in 1.

3   As in 1, let it "rain."
4   At "nose," touch it gently with fingertips. Stretch out the word "nose."

5   Lift hands up slowly.
6   As in 1 and 3, let it "rain."
7   At "toes," touch toes gently with fingertips. Stretch word "toes."

8   Lift hands slowly.
9   As in 1, let it "rain."
10 At "wet," starting with head, let it "rain down" all along the body, including

If the child sits on your lap hold her with one arm and let it "rain" with the other hand, that is, only with one hand.

The following play, "Rubbing Down," is an excellent complementary game in two ways:

I   Rain made the child wet, therefore she must be rubbed dry.

II "Rubbing down" complements the very gentle touches of this game with strong, hearty ones. The child can feel herself joyfully and announces her comfort with happy shouts.

arms and hands (gentle
touch with fingertips)
repeating the word: "wet"
till you have arrived at the
toes. 10 can be repeated,
but then, starting with the
head, let it "rain down"
the back.

Rubbing Down

RUBBA-RUBBA-RUBBA-ROWN,
I AM RUBBING BABY DOWN.
RUBBA-RUBBA-RUBBA-ROWN.
RUBBA-RUBBA-RUBBA-ROWN.
RUBBING DOWN MY BABY SWEET,
MUST BE DRY FROM HEAD TO FEET.
RUBBA-RUBBA-RUBBA-ROWN,
I AM RUBBING BABY DOWN.

IS ALL DRY?
FEET AND LEGS — THE BELLY ROUND —
HANDS AND ARMS — EARS AND NOSE —
HEAD — AND BACK ALL UP AND DOWN? —

DRY IS ALL! AND ALL IS DRY!
I TAKE MY BABY IN MY ARM
AND HOLD HER WUMMA-WUMMA-WARM!

TEXT:

1 Rubba-rubba-rubba-rown,
   I am rubbing baby down.
   Rubba-rubba-rubba-rown.
   Rubba-rubba-rubba-rown.
   Rubbing down my baby
                  sweet,
   Must be dry from head to
                     feet.
   Rubba-rubba-rubba-rown,
   I am rubbing baby down.

2 Is all dry?

GESTURES:

1 With your palms, rub the body of the child while reciting the verse rhythmically. Rub the various parts of the body in sequence. As you move from one part of the body to another, a small pause should occur. Generally speaking, the children love to be rubbed, even energetically. The adult, however, needs to be very aware how the child feels on a particular day, for what he enjoys one day may make him feel uncomfortable the next.

2 Stop and ask: Is all dry?

Perhaps, during the checking, the child may say that one part is not yet dry and wants it rubbed again. Then rub again saying, "Rubba-rubba-rubba-rown, I again will rub it down. So - now it's dry."

The "Rubbing Down" game can of course be played independently, without the rain game, "Drop-Drop-Droppeli," after washing or bathing or a real rain drenching, using a towel. Children who would otherwise object, will often allow themselves to be rubbed down energetically with this rhythmic verse. If you hold the child in your arm on your lap, rub down with one hand.

3 Feet and legs — the belly
                    round —
   Hands and arms — ears
                and nose —
   Head — and back all up
             and down? —

4 Dry is all! And all is dry!

5 I take my baby in my arm
6 And hold her wumma-
              wumma-warm!

3 Touch the parts of the
   body named in sequence
   to check if they are dry.
   Each time nod approving-
   ly. Touch gently, caressingly. After the energetic,
   enlivening rubbing the
   child needs to experience a
   comforting touch. End
   the game slowly.

4 Look at the child and
   affirm; nod at the
   word "dry."

5 Hug baby.
6 Rock baby to and fro in
   your arms for a while.

Round

ROUND — ROUND — ROUND, ALL, ALL ROUND.
BABY MINE IS SOUND.
SOUND, SOUND!

TEXT:

TOUCH:

1 Round —

1 Enclose the child's head lovingly with your own hands.

2 round —

2 Lay hands about the child's shoulders.

3 round,

3 Now lay hands on the child's tummy & pat a little.

4 all,

4 Lays hands on the child's knees.

5 all

5 Now put your hands on the child's calves and presses energetically.

6 round.

6 Finally, put your hands on the child's bottom and pat lightly.

7 Ba-
8 by
9 mine
10 is
11 sound.
12 Sound,
13 sound!

7 As in 1: head.
8 As in 2: shoulders.
9 As in 3: tummy.
10 As in 4: knees.
11 As in 5: calves.
12 As in 6: bottom.
13 Pat bottom twice or hug child in your arms.

PARTNER GAMES

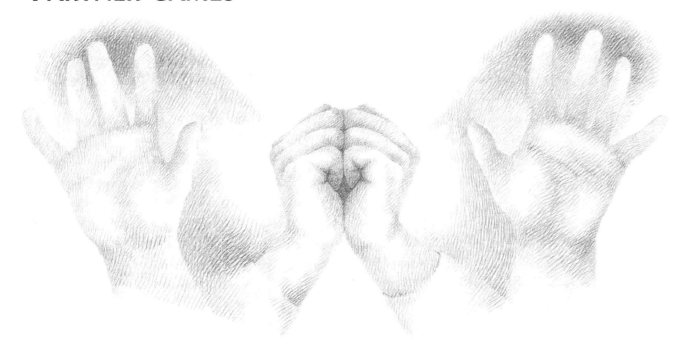

Dreaming of Snowing — of Snow

IT'S TIME THAT I TO BED MUST GO
TO SLEEP AND DREAM
OF SNOWING - OF SNOW!
HOW, IN MY DREAM, SNOWFLAKES LIGHT
FLOAT TO EARTH IN DARK OF NIGHT:
DOB! —
DOB! - DOB! —
DOB! - NOW HERE.
DOB! - NOW THERE.
DOB! - DOB! EVERYWHERE.
DOB! - DOB! FEATHER LIGHT.
DOB! - DOB! A DREAM AT NIGHT.
MOTHER STROKES HER BABY SWEET:
"SLEEP QUICKLY, DEAREST, GO TO SLEEP.
MY BABY DEAR, TO SLEEP YOU MUST GO,
THEN YOU CAN DREAM OF SNOWING - OF SNOW!" —

Directions for playing as hand gesture game:
(The adult plays the game on her own body).

TEXT:

1 It's time that I to bed must go

2 To sleep and dream
  Of snowing — of snow.

GESTURES:

1 Rest left cheek on joined palms, head slightly bent (symbolic gesture for sleeping) while rocking toward left with upper body.

2 With same gesture rock lightly to and fro, right, left, right.

This game can be played in two ways: in one version the adult demonstrates all hand gestures with and on her own body, so that the child can play along imitatively. In the other possible version the adult does the movements on the child, and the game becomes a touch game.

If the child has never experienced a touch game, the game "Dreaming of Snowing — of Snow" should only be played after the child is familiar with smaller, simpler caresses, such as "Aye-a - bye-a bocken" or "Ma-ma-moh."

62

3   How, in my dream,
                  snowflakes light
    Float to earth in dark of
                        night:

3   Lift both hands (palms fac-
    ing front). As all fingers
    move lightly and airily,
    move hands slowly down
    to head. It is snowing!
    Make this movement
    twice, touching on the
    head with your fingers at
    "light" and at "night."

4

4   With fingertips take turns
    touching body right and
    left very gently, barely per-
    ceptibly. It is important
    that the "b" at the end of
    "dob" sounds as a "b," not
    as a "p."

Dob!

Touch forehead with your
right fingertips.

Dob! — Dob!

Touch right cheek with
right, left cheek with left
fingertips.

Dob! — now here.

Touch nose, with right
hand, afterwards hand
makes an arc into the air.

Dob! — now there.

Touch chin, with right
hand, then again an arc in
the air.

Dob! — Dob!

Tap very lightly below col-
larbone, first right, then left.

                  everywhere.

Now tap right and left in
the breastbone region.

Dob! — Dob!

Tap right and left in the
chest region.

                  feather light.

Tap right and left in the
stomach region.

Dob! — Dob!

Tap right and left in the
navel region.

                  a dream at night.

Tap right and left in the
lower belly region. — After
a small pause continue:

5   Mother strokes her baby
                      sweet:

5   With right hand gently
    stroke down left arm from
    shoulder to fingertips.

6 "Sleep quickly, dearest, go to sleep.	6 With left hand stroke down right arm.
7 My baby dear, to sleep you must go,	7 With both hands at the same time stroke down head-temples-cheeks-chin.
8 Then you can dream	8 Join hands and make symbolic gesture for sleeping.

9 of snowing — of snow!"	9 Rock to and fro as in 2.

Directions for playing as touch game:

(The movements and touches are now carried out on the child).

TEXT:

GESTURES

Beginning: The child is put to bed.

1 My baby dear to bed
          must go

2 To sleep and dream
Of snowing - of snow.[1]

1 Rest your left cheek on joined palms, head slightly bent (symbolic gesture for sleeping) while rocking toward left with your upper body.

2 With same gesture rock lightly to and fro, right, left, right.

[1] Alternate beginning with corresponding text variances:

A The child already (ill) lies in bed (The movements are done by the adult with both hands).

  1 In her bed to sleep must go

  2 My child and dream of snowing - of snow.

B The adult holds the child in arm or on her lap (all movements and touches are done with one hand).

  1 In (on) my arm (lap) to sleep must go

  2 My child and dream of

3 How, in her dream,
                snowflakes light
   Float to earth in dark
                of night.

4 Dob! - Dob! (Continue
   with text as in 4, Self-
   touching Game)

5 Mother strokes her baby
                sweet:
   "Sleep quickly, dearest, go
                to sleep.

6 My baby dear, to sleep
                you must go,

7 Then you can dream of
                snowing - of snow."

8 Dob!

3 The movements for "snowing" are done in the same
   way as explained in the
   self-touching game at 3,
   depending on the situation
   with one or two hands.

4 As in the self-touching
   game, 4, touch child's
   body very gently with fingertips at the points
   described, with one or two
   hands, as the situation
   requires. If you have the
   impression that it benefits
   the child, or if the child
   asks for more, you can add
   more touches along with
   "dob," for example: knees
   and feet, or shoulders,
   elbows and hands.

5 Again, according to the situation, touch the child
   with both hands at the
   same time or only with
   one hand: stroke twice
   from shoulders across
   arms, once per line of text.

6 Stroke from head across
   temples and cheeks down
   to the chin, at the same
   time with both hands or
   with one hand only.

7 Hold the child's face very
   lightly in both hands or
   only one hand.

8 Touch tip of nose very
   lightly. Rest hand gently
   on head or cheek for a
   short while.

snowing - of snow.

C The child sits across from
   the adult (again the adult
   can make the movement and
   touches with both hands):

1 I play that you to bed
                must go

2 To sleep and dream of
                snowing - of snow.

1 We play that now to bed
                we go

2 And sleep and dream of
                snowing - of snow.

The touches must be very
gentle; they represent snow
flakes, not rain drops. If the
child lies covered in bed, the
adult can perform the touches
on the coverlet. The child will
still perceive them. The movements should be very slow to
give the experience of floating.

Glitz — Glitz and Thaws Away

SNOWFLAKES ARE FLOATING FROM HEAVEN FREE
SOFTLY DOWN ON LAND AND SEA.
ONE LANDS ON MY HEAD! LOOK! – I SAY
GOES GLITZ — GLITZ AND THAWS AWAY.

SNOWFLAKES ARE FLOATING FROM HEAVEN FREE
SOFTLY DOWN ON LAND AND SEA.
ONE LANDS ON MY CHEST! LOOK – I SAY
GOES GLITZ — GLITZ AND THAWS AWAY.

SNOWFLAKES ARE FLOATING FROM HEAVEN FREE
SOFTLY DOWN ON LAND AND SEA.
ONE LANDS ON MY KNEE! LOOK! – I SAY
GOES GLITZ — GLITZ AND THAWS AWAY.

SNOWFLAKES ARE FLOATING FROM HEAVEN FREE
SOFTLY DOWN ON LAND AND SEA.
ONE LANDS ON MY HAND! LOOK! – I SAY
GOES GLITZ — GLITZ AND THAWS AWAY.

SNOWFLAKES ARE FLOATING FROM HEAVEN FREE
SOFTLY DOWN ON LAND AND SEA.
ONE LANDS ON MY NOSE! LOOK! – I SAY
GOES GLITZ — GLITZ AND THAWS AWAY.

SNOWFLAKES ARE FLOATING FROM HEAVEN FREE
SOFTLY DOWN ON LAND AND SEA.
DOWN TO THE EARTH THE SNOWFLAKES FLY
AND THERE THEY LIE.

TEXT:

1   Snowflakes are floating
           from heaven free
    Softly down on land and
                          sea.

GESTURES:

1   Both hands are snowflakes.
    Each hand, fingers and
    thumb loosely bent, palm
    down, form a little para-
    chute. Move parallel hands
    down, airily, in little arcs
    up and down and to and

Include any ideas the children volunteer on where else
the snowflake lands.
   This game can also be played
as a partner game. Then
change the text: "One lands
on your head!"

66

2   One lands on my head!

3   Look! — I say

4   Goes glitz — glitz

5   and thaws away.

fro. Start movement as high as forehead moving down to middle of chest.

2   The right hand (little parachute) is now the "one snowflake" rising on the word "one" slowly vertically above the head. Speak slowly. Slowly the snowflake floats down again and at the word "head" the snowflake, now as a loose fist, touches down on the head on the thumb.

3   Without wrinkling forehead look in the snowflake's direction.

4   Spread out fingers of the right hand twice toward the audience.

5   On the side of the thumb let the loose fist glide from head to temple and down the cheek.

6   Snowflakes are floating…
                  etc.

7   One lands on… etc.

8   Down to the earth the
         snowflakes fly

9   And there they lie.

6   For the refrain use movements described in 1.

7   Again use only the right hand for the snowflake. In sequence it lands on chest, knee, hand and nose. When it thaws, glide the loose fist down from the described place for a bit. Allow yourself time.

8   Hands now move in snowflake gesture to thigh or to the floor. Let hands lie loosely on thighs or floor.

9   Look at them for a while, then continue with an affirmative nod.

Boom and Botch

BOOM AND BOTCH AND
WOOM AND WATCH AND
BOB AND BAW AND
HERE AND DAW AND
TRALLALALLALALLALA!
AND HOOH AND MOO
AND OPP AND TOO! — YEA!

TEXT:

MOVEMENTS:

*See "Movements," page 19

1   Boom and

1   With both fists (thumbs on the outside) thump lightly and springily on thighs.

2   Botch and

2   Lightly & springily clap hands.

3   Woom and

3   With flat hands (fingertips forward) wipe energetically forward along thighs, from legs to knees.

4   Watch and

4   and backwards again.

5   Bob and Baw and

5   Springily clap together fists (upright, with fingers rolled in. Thumbs lie on the rolled-in pointers*). At the slow "Baw" turn fists while opening hands wide (fingers splayed) so one sees the palms. Hold a while.

6   Here and

6   With fingertips of both hands tip against chest (height of breast bone).

7   Daw and

7   With hands (palms down) point far ahead without overstretching.

8 Trallalallalallala! — and

8 Turn lifted hands in and out.

9 Hooh and

9 Hold hands beside mouth as a "megaphone" without touching. Call "Hooh" slowly, not too loud.

10 Moo and

10 With pinkies touching lay hands together in front of your mouth and call into them a deep "moo."

11 Opp and

11 Open arms as for a hug.

12 Too! —

12 Cross hands over chest, right hand across left. For children older then five years you can let your fingers disappear, the right hand under the left armpit, the left hand under the right armpit.

13 — Yea! —

13 Move hands down in a small arc. Lay them flat on thighs after an affirmative nod at the word "yea." Sit quietly for a while.

Verses For Babes In Arms

These verses are meant for the very small child. Mother or Father holds the child and stands, for instance, at the window, on the veranda, in the garden or even in a park or in the woods. Hold the child with one arm, leaving the other free to carry out the gestures and motions.

As early as possible, children should be led to perceive natural sounds around them. It is especially important in the city, or in a household with the noises of machinery, that the child's ear be attuned to the voices of nature. The joy that the child feels when looking up to the stars or hearing the song of the birds disposes her toward a feeling of gratitude later in life. It develops the capacity to receive comfort, for example, through hearing bird-song in difficult life situations. Love for the earth is developed and with it the need to guard and protect it.

All The Dear Stars

(For the melody to this song, see "Songs for Children," page 94)

ALL THE DEAR STARS iN THE HEAVENS FREE

DOWN THEY ARE GAZiNG ON LAND AND SEA,

TWiNKLE iN DARKNESS WiTH SHiMMERiNG RAY.

WHO CAN, DEAR STARS, WHO YOUR NUMBERS CAN SAY?

ALL THE DEAR STARS iN THE HEAVENS FREE

DOWN THEY ARE GAZiNG ON LAND AND SEA.

TEXT:

1 All the dear stars in the heavens free

2 Down they are gazing on land and sea,

3 Twinkle in darkness with shimmering ray.

4 Who can, dear stars, who your numbers can say?

5 All the dear stars in the heavens free

6 Down they are gazing on land and sea.

7 (Silent movement)

PLAY DIRECTION:

1 With baby in arm step to the window and, with your free hand, slowly point up to the stars.

2 Slowly lower your free hand pointing out into the world.

3 With your hand describe a semicircle above to show the vault of heaven.

4 Make a similar semi-circular movement with your hand in the opposite direction.

5 Movement as in 1.

6 Movement as in 2.

7 Lightly stroke the child's cheek hugging her gently. Do this silently.

A Little Bird Sits in a Tree

A little bird sits in a tree
Too small, too small for you to see.
But we all hear it call!
Cheep-cheeeep! — Cheep-cheeeep! — Cheep-cheeeep!
It sings: Hear! — Hear!
Cheep-cheeeep! — Cheep-cheeeep! —
"Little one, You are my dear!"

TEXT:

1 A little bird sits in a tree
2 Too small, too small for
      you to see.

3 But we all hear it call!

4 Cheep-cheeeep! —
      Cheep-cheeeep! —
      Cheep-cheeeep!

5 It sings. Hear! — Hear!
6 Cheep-cheeeep! — Cheep
      cheeeep!
   "Little one, You are my
      dear!"

PLAY DIRECTIONS:

1 Point to the tree.
2 Touch forehead with your
   hand, looking for the
   birdie in the tree branches.
3 Hold your hand to
   your ear and listen for
   the singing.
4 Thumb and pointer*
   touch each other as beak.
   The other fingers are
   rolled in.   Open the beak
   at the "ee" of the word
   "cheep" and shut it again
   at "p" of the word "cheep."
5 Listen, as in 3.
6 Again open and shut beak
   in speech rhythm.

Ending: Stroke the child's
cheek lovingly or press his
head against you while saying:
"And mine, too."

*See "Movements," page 19

My Heart Beats:
"Bum — Bum — Bum!"

Father or Mother may hold the child lovingly in arm and softly speak to her the following text:

I HOLD YOU IN MY ARM;
YOU LIE THERE SOFT AND WARM.
UPON MY HEART YOUR HEAD YOU LAY —
"BUM - BUM - BUM!", YOU HEAR IT SAY.
LISTEN NOW, MY LITTLE DOVE:
"BUM — BUM — BUM!", SO SOUNDS
MY LOVE."
"BUM — BUM — BUM!", SO SOUNDS
MY LOVE."

In Father's Arm

Mother sits with the child in her arms, Father stands behind them embracing them both. Mother speaks the verse:

FATHER ENFOLDS US IN HIS ARM;
WITH HIS HAND HOLDS BABY SURE.
BOTH MOTHER AND HER BABY FINE —
IN HIS EMBRACE MAY FEEL SECURE.

IN FATHER'S ARM
IT IS SO WARM!

Lullabies

Rocking

At the Loom of Time

When a mother her baby is rocking,
See through the window the moon

shining clear —
And when heaven the earth is loving,
That's when a mother rocks her baby dear.

Gottfried Wolters

At birth, the child enters the space where gravity holds sway, and we are called upon again and again to offer for his or her well-being on the hard road to earth existence, the feeling of weightlessness. An especially good and effective means for this is rocking. To be rocked is in some degree a continuation of the feeling of rocking and being carried that the child experienced while yet unborn in the mother's womb as she walked the earth.

Moreover we need to remember that the child, surrounded and carried before birth in the watery element within the placenta, feels afterwards surrounded by air — the new element that carries tone and sound to the ear, indeed to the whole body structure.

Sounds, muffled to perception within the womb, are replaced by the experience of clear tones. Familiar sounds from the womb are reborn on a new level in the mother's singing. Thus rocking and singing belong together. There is nothing that small children, and also bigger ones, are so fond of as being rocked while being hummed or sung to. They prosper as though fed an especially nutritious food — a heavenly food.

Rocking, with the sound of voice and speech, is like a delicious nourishment. It is the bread and water of life that we bring the children.

Through the mother's voice the child is united with the world. Just as before birth the child was united with the mother by the umbilical cord, so after birth it is in large measure the mother's voice, so to speak a voice cord, that now unites the child with the mother, and through her with living on earth, where he wants to develop.

This bond is established in an especially intimate and profound way when the mother sings as she rocks. This is evidenced through countless lullabies. Every era has recognized the child's need for rocking. Cradles and rocking-chairs were built and hammocks strung, yet nothing is so well-suited, so protective and enfolding as mother's lap or father's arm. The warmth of bodily contact is of great significance. Above all it is the place where the child lies at the mother's heart, hearing her heartbeat not only with his ear, but with his entire organism. Just as in the uterus before birth, after birth the child feels most protected in his mother's lap. (The noted author of children's books, Jakob Streit, tells that in Switzerland the common expression describing a harmonious, well balanced person is that as a child he was "well-rocked.")

To have a newborn swim in water in order to give the feeling of weightlessness, as in the amniotic fluid, or to play tapes to the child of the sounds of circulation and heartbeat heard within the mother's body, is not what the child needs after he is born. Even though the child may be calmed by such an appeal to its prenatal memories, we need to be aware that this is a return to a part of life already overcome, already outgrown. A new approach needs to be found and given for the present and future form of being in order to fit the new bodily expectations. Electronic media don't meet this need.[1] In order to satisfy the child's bodily needs, it is important throughout the first seven years, but especially in the first three years, to make possible the healthy formation of the body as the basis for the development of soul and mind.

On mother's lap, the child rests on his mother's heart. In the lullabies he feels the heartbeat on a higher level through well-formed speech and poetic rhythm. The constant repetition of similarities in the stress of speech and the experience of pulsation in song evokes a feeling of security within the child. Through rhyme, trust is strengthened. When at the end of two lines two syllables harmonize in the same sound, this fact is experienced throughout the whole body. It is like the fulfillment of a joyful expectation, for one can count on its recurring every time. This develops confidence. Literal meaning doesn't matter; it is the harmony or sound in its balancing effect that counts. To meet artistically formed speech in lullabies is to know security on a higher level. Speech is spiritual reality. In meeting it the child feels the presence of lap and enveloping protection, a home, as it were, transformed into a higher being.

A child is a person who needs to and wants to grow up; he needs a protected space in which to develop while being shielded from the adult world. This is especially true regarding the music the child hears. At birth the harmony of the spheres had to be left behind, yet the music of the planets still resounds within. A reflection can be found here on earth in music created by human beings. The child under the age of seven can experience only a small part of the full range of the twelve-tone series of intervals of the fifth. This smaller range is called the "mood of the fifth" with central tone A. The child can be active within this "tonal space" in a beneficial way, as in it he still lives closely connected with the cosmos. By way of this tonal space a "safe enclosure" is formed wherein the child can rest as in the lap of the stars. It is an unclouded, emotion-free space of security, lifted out of all earthly unrest, comparable to our experience when, gazing at ancient icons with their gold background, we may feel ourselves embraced by the warm glow as in a veil of light that surrounds and protects us. It is important to consider all this when composing the melodies for lullabies.

When one becomes fully aware of how very much the child is exposed to conventional contemporary music, one should feel called upon to provide as often and as much as possible a different kind of tonal space, a sort of "protected realm," for the beginning of life's sojourn on earth.

Whoever wants to know the full blossom and wholesome fruit cannot get around providing for the plant a healthy, strengthening soil for it to take root and grow. For that reason, what is here presented is intended to be a "model" of lullabies for voice as well as for instruments such as those provided by Choroi, tuned in fifths with central tone A. These songs have proven themselves over decades at home, in kindergartens and orphanages, as well as in workshops with mother and child groups in rhythmic-musically formed game-units. The rest periods embedded in the games were felt to have profound healing qualities. It is hoped that both the songs and the use of elementary Choroi instruments will stimulate parents, teachers, curative educators and others in the healing professions to choose and try out whatever fits their own situations, at the same time encouraging them to create their own melodies and texts in the same sense as those presented here.

[1]See "Tonal Quality of Electronic Apparatus," page 80

The Experience of Rhythm in the First Seven Years of Childhood

The feeling of rhythm in the first seven years is fundamental, based on pulsation. Pulsation is the initial element, the germinal cell of all rhythmic activity. It is the constant repetition of what is similar, yet not identical. Pulsation is the basic beat, oriented to the heartbeat, dividing the stream of time.

Pulsation has two aspects: it is the polarity between stress and relief, impulse and relaxation (usually denoted as "pause" or "rest"), in which something decisive occurs, namely the preparation for another impulse. The heartbeat also has two parts: a polarity of expansion and contraction (systole and diastole); in the same way, breathing has its polarity of exhalation and inhalation. Like pulse and breathing, pulsation is variable in tempo; like these it has an elastic ability to adjust and can become slower or faster, thus working as an enlivening element in time's flow. Pulsation forms the basis for all ordering of time.

In spite of the action of its movement, there is nothing merely mechanical about pulsation. It has nothing to do with the usual time counting music teachers use to accustom their pupils to a regular tempo, often with the well-known mechanical metronome as its basis. This mechanical metrical tempo measurement is a linear, non-living rate per second in which the "beat" is hammered out, partitioning, but carrying no

forward movement such as one finds in the stress of pulsation. Through the metrical time-measure, all living streaming and breathing is destroyed. It has a deadly effect on all musical execution.

The precision of pulsation is different from that of the machine. It responds not to mechanical laws, but to those of life. Therefore it is not fixed, or monotonous; it is elastic in its constant alternation between phases of stress and relief.

Graphically illustrated:

Meter: ▬ ▬ ▬ ▬ ▬ ▬ ▬ ▬ ▬ ▬ ▬ ▬ ▬

Beat: ● ▬ ▬ ● ▬ ▬ ● ▬ ▬ ● ▬ ▬ ● ▬ ▬ ▬

Pulsation ∿∿∿∿∿∿∿∿∿∿∿∿∿

In the first seven years of life, the blood circulation and breathing only gradually become coordinated. A rhythmic relationship only slowly becomes established and stable. (This process actually only comes to its final equilibrium around the ninth year of life.) For this reason, one should spare children in this stage of life the rule of measure, beat, and fixed note value, for these are a harmful, disturbing, even destructive interference for the child.

Movement, speech and song should be brought to the child as pulsating activity in support of the building up of the bodily organism and its functions. This especially concerns the lullabies.

Mood Of The Fifth
With Central Tone A

Pentatonic melodies can only move in a swinging motion around a central tone. They float, without a stressed beginning and without tending toward a resolved end. They expand in a spiral or in increasing struggle and constantly swing back within their own boundaries. They play with tones and are intoning play.

Fritz Jöde

Mood of the fifth with central tone A corresponds to the cosmic experience of the child in the first seven years, who still is at one with the world and does not yet feel a polarity between it and himself. This musical mode forms a protective shelter in which the child can feel secure.

Mood of the fifth signifies unity with the cosmos, in which heavens and earth are yet united. It means being in harmony with a divine center.

It is a tonal space of optimal balance. All tones of the upper and lower fifth intervals are equally far removed from the central tone A. The entire space comprises not an octave but a ninth-interval in which everything is in balance.

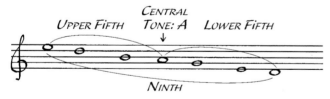

Pentatonic mood of the fifth (original ancient Greek form) with central tone A

The diatonic scale has a different structure: there are two centers. Contrast is established between the fundamental tone and its octave. Half-tones, minor and major thirds give rise to minor and major modes with their respective feminine and masculine characters. From this springs the phenomenon of duality with the world, contrasting with the unity achieved through the mood of the fifth. In the songs for the first seven years of life, this duality should not yet be broached.

The entrance of the third, major and minor, makes it possible for the human being to come to know his inner life, to comprehend himself within his feeling. This offers the possibility of imposing limits on oneself, which represents progress in development. It is not hard to see how harm can ensue if the tendency for self-limitation is promoted in a child, for whom unity with the world is the needed basis for healthy development.

In the lullabies this need of the children is fully and entirely considered. According to manifold experience, the exclusive presentation of mood of the fifth motifs and melodies, brings about a profound recovery and healing from the harmful influences to which the child is exposed in his or her surroundings.

Mood of the fifth -- tonal space:

with the central tone A in its play about this central tone,

approximates the sound-gesture of rocking and brings about a dreaming, floating state of consciousness in the child. Sinking into the lower fifth interval

supports exhalation, yet allows return to the central A without too much heaviness, allowing freedom.

The experience of a light, floating sensation is supported by an upward climbing line:

in order to avoid "floating away," a gravitational counterpoise is given through final return to central tone A

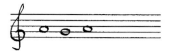

or through a play in second intervals around the central tone:

Carrying out the Games with Children whose Behavior is Disturbed

One thing must be noted. Whatever is offered to the children in the lullabies in mood of the fifth with central tone A is a gift to us from the spirit world, given creative form.

What works spiritually in speech and body gestures is something into which children, but also adults, can immerse themselves as into a healing bath. There are both children and grown-ups who live in this as in their life-element and thus prosper. Others only enter in haltingly, and some may even refuse to enter.

In that case: Patience! Those who don't make it are basically very unhappy, for they would really be only too glad to participate, but life and environment have already placed many barriers and hindrances in their way which one must carefully dismantle and help place in order. That is just what takes place through these songs in the mood of the fifth, which through rhythm and tune carry the ordering element of the creative world (activity of the stars) to the child.

It is essential not to let oneself become irritated by the destructive misbehavior of these upset children, who most especially need this help. Don't regard these difficulties as disturbances; instead, avoid reacting angrily. We must be filled with deep compassion for children so strongly traumatized by their environment; only one thought should motivate us, namely to help them find again their way to the healing spring from which they have been cut off.

Have no expectations; do not in any way preconceive what the child is expected or required to do. Let the child sit quietly or play somewhere by him- or herself. On the other hand, always carry the child in your consciousness throughout the whole process. There will be moments in which the child's attention is caught, when he may even come over and want to participate in what you are doing. Cymbals, Choroi harp or flute may be the lure. The child listens to the gentle tone and clings to its caress. Increasingly he or she is drawn into what is being done, and child and adult can gradually relax. It is really like a release from shackles.

People working together must lend each other strength in sustaining this approach in order for it to eventually bear fruit. The problems will recede, maybe even be solved. A peacefulness enters that fills both child and adult with joy and thanksgiving, and gives strength to solve the next problem.

Tonal Quality of Electronic Apparatus

The question of using electronic apparatus for sound production and reproduction answers itself when the following is considered:

What is lacking for the child in media experience is the encounter with the "I" or self of another human being. There also is no human "you to you" relationship on the psychological or soul level or bodily contact on the physical level. The child knows no real security. As an example, one mother's report follows:

A child, sitting on his mother's lap, had always had a bedtime story told and was rocked while mother sang a lullaby. On his fourth birthday he was given a compact disc with good-night stories and lullabies. The mother, wanting to give her child more varied bedtime fare, hoped secretly to save herself some time. Thereafter she played the disc for her child to go to sleep by. Soon, however, the initial interest of the child waned, and he asked mother to sit with him and sing and tell stories. The mother, on the other hand, failed to understand, thinking the stories and songs on the compact disc were told and sung much better than she could do it, and even had instrumental accompaniment!

The child meanwhile insisted on rejecting all that and retained his fervent wish for his mother to sit and sing and rock him. After much questioning: "Oh, but why? What's the reason?" finally he said: "The disc doesn't have a lap!" The child was going away empty-handed from his bodily expectations. He was being given "stones for bread." His soul's hunger for tenderness was not being satisfied by the CD.

As to the tonal quality and sound transmitted by such apparatus, attention needs to be paid to the fact that one is faced with an illusion. This is explained in the following citation from Ernst Marti's book, *The Etheric*:

"Today's acoustic theory does not take 'tone ether' into account. It is convinced that tone is produced solely by physical-mechanical factors; a string of defined weight, length and tension, and a finger to pluck it; a bell of definite material and configuration, with a clapper to strike it; etc. Only purely physical facts. This view became the main reason for the materialistic conception of sense perception. Physically generated and transmitted air waves were thought to be both cause and essence of tone. From this beginning, our entire perceived world was declared to be the result of wave motion and nothing but wave motion.

"This notion is fundamentally incorrect! Rudolf Steiner pointed out the error of this theory in his introduction to Goethe's writings on natural science. He explained the actual relation of physical air vibration to tone as an etheric effect. Vibrations are present in the physical world. They make it possible for the tone-ether, itself supersensible, to enter into the sensible world and be perceived as tone. Without vibrations there is no tone! We do not hear vibrations but the related tone ether, expressed in the quality of a particular tone, such as A or D for example.

"Thus it is possible for us human beings to produce vibrations in order for a tone to ensue. That is an ability which shows us human beings our responsibility for the tonality within the world if we become aware of it. Vibration is the body of the tone, in which the tone-ether works. Just consider the difference in tone's body if it is produced by the breath through a flute, or through an electronic organ or a radio. One can see how different the tonal quality is, and thus how different its effect upon the world."[1]

And I should like to add: And above all its effect on small children. Those fine ears are still so close to their creator; they still hear the sound of the heavens. This connection to the cosmos should be maintained as long as possible in order that the children continue to hear in tones and sounds the sound of the starry world, undiminished through electrical manipulation that makes a connection to the cosmos difficult or impossible. At this stage of life, we should bring to the children the protective care given even in our industrial society to young plants so that they remain directly connected to the etheric stream of life.

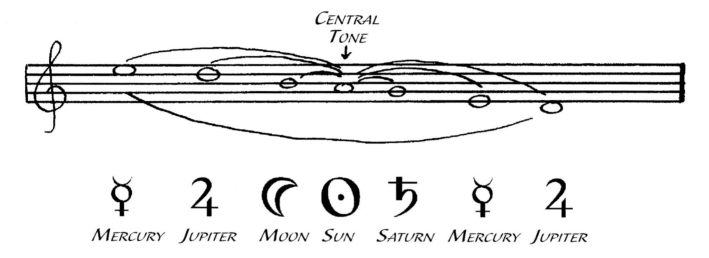

CENTRAL TONE

MERCURY   JUPITER   MOON   SUN   SATURN   MERCURY   JUPITER

[1] Ernst Marti: *The Etheric — Eine Erweiterung der Naturwissenschaft durch Anthroposophie;* published by Irmgard Rossmann, Dornach, Switzerland, 1994.

The Practice of Singing

It needs to be mentioned that the adult should approach the child very carefully with lullabies and melodic motifs. Singing should be *sotto voce* without vibrato. The tone glides on the breath stream, surrounding rather than gripping the child. The rocking movement and the singing of the words must be embedded in a pulsating flow.[1] The singing is not meant to impress, but to form a shelter into which the child can nestle. To do this, all sentimentality and emphasis on the textual meaning need to be avoided. The flow of sound is to be given objectively, making possible the feeling of cosmic order.

Tuning the voice

If one is not sure of being able to sing an A freely by ear, one may avail oneself of one of the Choroi instruments: interval flute, brass tone bar, kinderharp. Calmly play the tone A to the children, then humming or singing "la-la," let the tone continue. Singing the tone A to the children is essential; it engages them in the tonality and provides the needed basis for singing.

[1] See "The Experience of Rhythm," p. 77

General Remarks on Notation

The central tone A referred to is the A above middle C. The notes do not represent fixed note values based on measurable time lengths. They are meant as memory aids for the melodies. Sing freely, following the motion of language and movement, not being necessarily bound by long or short notes or time-beat. The flow of speech determines the rhythmic and dynamic movement.

● ≈ a basic unit: the pulsation oriented to the heartbeat, in the streaming, swinging musical flow, without a time-beat indicated by stress or firmly bound to note length.

Singing should follow the rhythm of speech, calm, possibly slowing at the end. In playing instruments as well, follow a free rhythm in the melodies, giving emphasis where the text asks for it.

The tempo, whether sung or played on an instrument, is determined not only by the song's character, but also depends on the situation in which it is sung or played. If previous play has been lively, start by picking up the song somewhat faster, gradually leading into a calm mood. If already calm, one can start slower. With restless or nervous children, a faster basic tempo is needed than for calm natured children. Parents and care-givers must develop a fine sensibility in order to accommodate each individual situation or possibility. That means: practice — practice — practice!

In the singing of lullabies to a child in the first seven years the same holds true as in the rest of life. Parents and caregivers must above all prepare themselves, in order to "be" that which they want to present to the children. Then the child can imitate and breathe along with that which leads to calmness. We need to be aware of, and should joyfully accept, our responsibility. Having the children become, to use the Swiss folk expression "well-rocked," is well worth the effort needed on our part to develop and perfect new capacities.

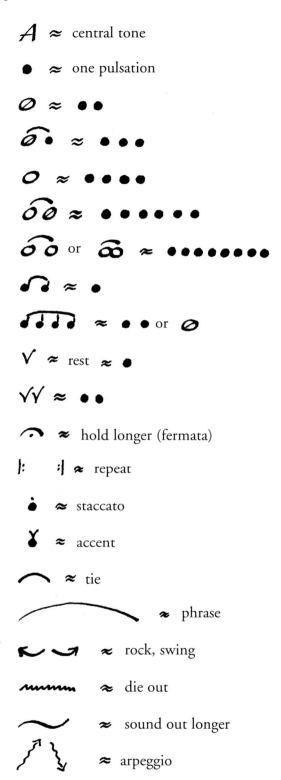

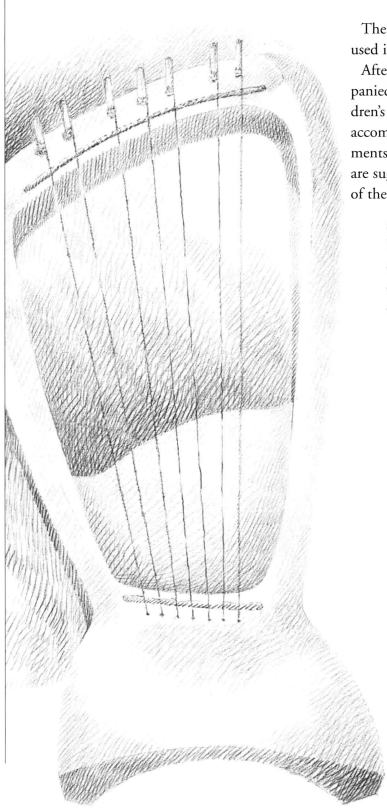

SONGS FOR CHILDREN

The lullabies and songs for quiet time can be used in many play situations.

After lively circle games, a period of rest accompanied by a lullaby brings harmony into the children's play. Songs for quiet time may also be accompanied on single stringed or metal instruments or by hand gestures. Various possibilities are suggested for the following songs by insertion of the key letters a - e next to the song title.

a = suitable for rest pauses within a game
b = also intended for Choroi flute
c = to play or accompany on kinder harp
d = to accompany with metal instruments
e = with hand gestures

Rocka-Rocka-Bye-A

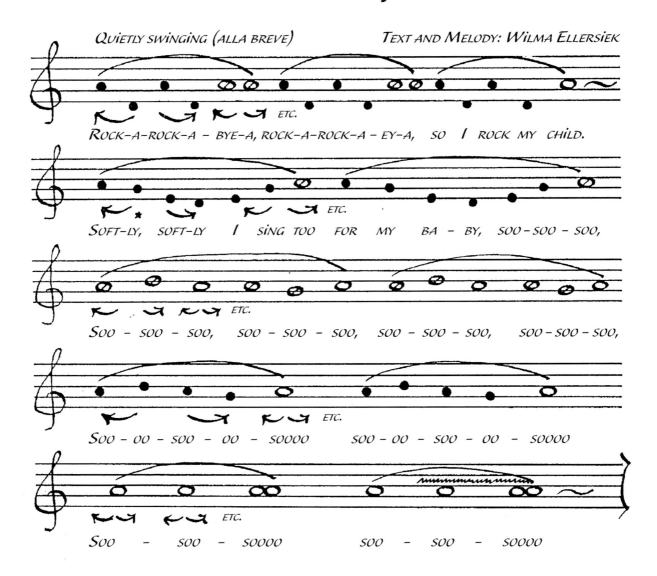

Quietly swinging (alla breve) *Text and Melody: Wilma Ellersiek*

Rock-a-rock-a - bye-a, rock-a-rock-a - ey-a, so / rock my child.

Soft-ly, soft-ly / sing too for my ba - by, soo-soo - soo,

Soo - soo - soo, soo - soo - soo, soo - soo - soo, soo - soo - soo,

Soo - oo - soo - oo - soooo soo - oo - soo - oo - soooo

Soo - soo - soooo soo - soo - soooo

NOTATION: Ø ≈ A SLOW PULSATION (BASIC UNIT) / • • ≈ Ø FOR A SLOW PULSATION TWO NOTES IN A MIDDLE TEMPO / O ≈ ØØ / OO ≈ ØØØØ / ~ ≈ SOUND OUT LONGER / ⌇⌇⌇ ≈ LET IT DIE OUT, AT THE SAME TIME SLOWER AND SOFTER / ⌒ ≈ ONE BREATH / ↶↷ ≈ ROCKING

*INSTEAD OF "I" ONE CAN NAME THE PERSON WHO ROCKS THE BABY. FOR EXAMPLE: "MOTHER ROCKS HER CHILD"

Evening Wind

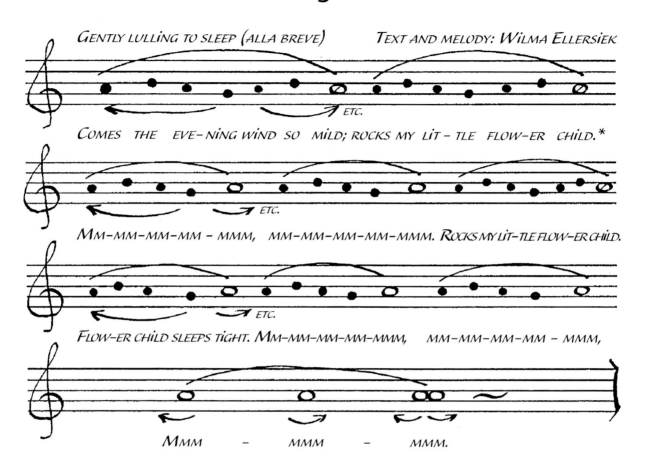

Gently lulling to sleep (alla breve)   Text and melody: Wilma Ellersiek

Comes the eve-ning wind so mild; rocks my lit-tle flow-er child.*

Mm-mm-mm-mm - mmm, mm-mm-mm-mm-mmm. Rocks my lit-tle flow-er child.

Flow-er child sleeps tight. Mm-mm-mm-mm-mmm, mm-mm-mm-mm - mmm,

Mmm - mmm - mmm.

*Instead of "flower child" one can sing "dearest little child," or one can name various animals: "beetle child, birdie child" etc.

Notation: Ø ≈ a slow pulsation (basic unit) | • • ≈ Ø for a slow pulsation two notes in a middle tempo | O ≈ ØØ | ⊂⊃ ≈ ØØØØ | ~ ≈ extend the sound | ⌇⌇⌇ ≈ let it die out, at the same time slower and softer | ⌒ ≈ one breath | ↩ ↪ ≈ rocking

Father Rocks His Baby

SOFT AND TENDER (ALLA BREVE)　　　　TEXT AND MELODY: WILMA ELLERSIEK

1) A —— AH!　A —— AH!
2) A —— AH!　A —— AH!
3) A —— AH!　A —— AH!
4) A —— AH!　A —— AH!
5) A —— AH!　A —— AH!

1) ROCKS THE WIND THE TREE ____
   ROCKS THE TREE THE BIRD - IE.

2) ROCKS THE BROOK THE BOAT ____
   AND WHO ROCKS MY BA - BY?

3) FA - THER ROCKS HIS BA - BY,
   AS THE BROOK THE BOAT ____

4) AS THE TREE THE BIRD - IE.
   AS THE WIND THE TREE ____ .

5) SO HE ROCKS HIS BA - BY
   TILL SHE FALLS A - SLEEP ____ .

6) A —— AH!　A —— AH!

6) A —— AH!　A —— AH!

NOTATION: ⊘ ≈ ONE SLOW PULSATION (BASIC UNIT) / •• ≈ ⊘ FOR A SLOW PULSATION TWO NOTES IN A MIDDLE TEMPO / ○ ≈ ⊘⊘ / ∞ ≈ ⊘⊘⊘⊘ (: :) ≈ REPEAT / ∼ ≈ SOUND OUT LONGER / ⌇⌇⌇ ≈ DYING OUT, AT THE SAME TIME GROWING SLOWER AND SOFTER / ⌒ ≈ ONE BREATH / ↶↷ ≈ ROCKING

Shoo! — Off to Bed

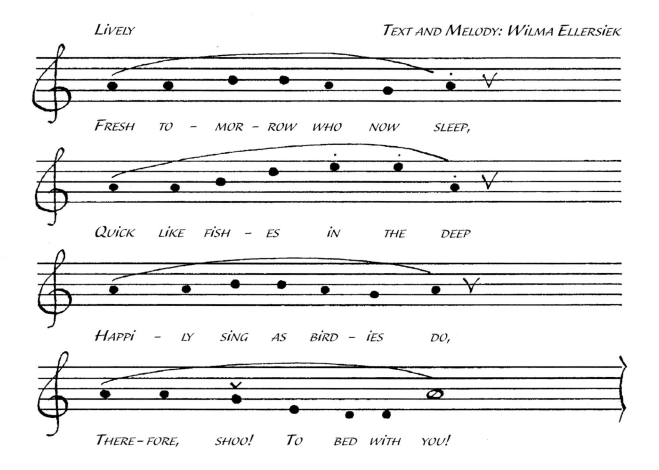

Lively

Text and Melody: Wilma Ellersiek

Fresh to - mor - row who now sleep,

Quick like fish - es in the deep

Happi - ly sing as bird - ies do,

There - fore, shoo! To bed with you!

Notation: ● ≈ *a pulsation (basic unit)* | ⊘ ≈ ●● | V ≈ ● *rest* | v ≈ *stress* | ● ≈ *short (staccato)* | ⌒ ≈

This song is very suitable to prepare the child to go to bed, undress, wash, etc.

As a friendly, musical encouragement it has often been helpful in situations when the children don't want to stop their play.

Rest — Diddledoo (a, b)

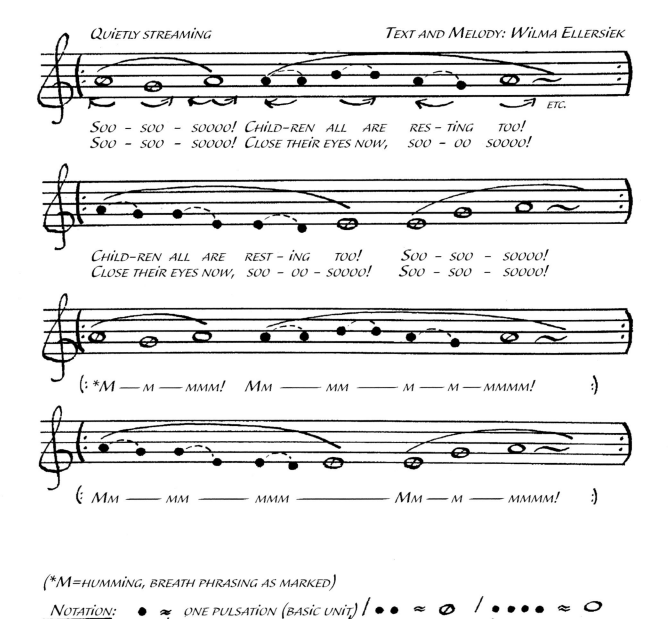

Quietly streaming   Text and Melody: Wilma Ellersiek

Soo - soo - soooo! Child-ren all are res - ting too!
Soo - soo - soooo! Close their eyes now, soo - oo soooo!

Child-ren all are rest - ing too! Soo - soo - soooo!
Close their eyes now, soo - oo - soooo! Soo - soo - soooo!

(: *M — m — mmm! Mm ——— mm ——— m — m — mmmm!   :)

(: Mm ——— mm ——— mmm ——— Mm — m ——— mmmm!   :)

(*M=humming, breath phrasing as marked)

Notation: ● ≈ one pulsation (basic unit) / ●● ≈ ⌀ / ●●●● ≈ ◯
(: :) ≈ repeat / ‿ ≈ one breath / ↶↷ ≈ rocking / ~ ≈ let it die out

Through the year "Rest-diddledoo" accompanies many periods of rest. It is a basic gesture of exhaling. It is important that the tone lightly glides along on the breath stream, whether it is sung, hummed or played on the flute. Particularly at the end of a phrase the tone must remain suspended, so that it is not oppressive.

The tempo of this song depends on the preceding play situation. Sing faster after a lively playtime than after a quiet one. We have to adjust. If the song was started in a lively way slow the tempo down a bit during singing.

When "Rest-diddledoo" is played on the pentatonic Choroi flute, all short notes are either tied or slurred; (dotted ties). Each note is not attacked separately; just add a gentle increase in the breath stream.

While Moon and Stars are Shining

QUIETLY NARRATING   *TEXT AND MELODY: WILMA ELLERSIEK*

1) THE MOON STANDS IN THE HEAV - ENS FREE_____
   LOOK - ING DOWN ON LAND AND SEA, SHE

2) THE STARS STAND IN THE HEAV - ENS FREE_____
   LOOK - ING DOWN ON LAND AND SEA, THEY

3) FOR ALL THE NIGHT IN DARK - NESS DEEP_____
   MOON AND STARS THEIR WARD DO KEEP, THEY

1) SHINES ON MY BA - BY DEAR!

2) GLEAM FOR MY BA - BY DEAR!

3) WATCH FOR MY BA - BY DEAR!

4) WHILE MOON AND STARS ARE SHIN - ING CLEAR /
   PUT TO BED MY BA - BY DEAR. NOW

4) SLEEP, BA - BY SLEEP. NOW SLEEP, — NOW SLEEP, — NOW SLEEP!

NOTATION: ● ≈ ONE PULSATION (BASIC UNIT) | ⊘ ≈ ●● | ⊘͡● ≈ ●●● | ⊘ ≈ ●●●●
~ ≈ HOLD LONGER | (: :) ≈ REPEAT | V ≈ BRAKE | ⌇⌇⌇ ≈ DYING OUT, AT THE SAME TIME
GROWING SLOWER AND SOFTER | ⌒ ≈ ONE BREATH

This song is intended for the very young child once he has discovered the moon and later the stars.

As you carry him in your arms, first sing only Verse 1 about the moon followed by Verse 3 ("the silver moon her ward does keep"); change in Verse 4 ("while silver moon is shining clear…") Later, one can add Verse 2. One can sing the song also without Verse 4. Parents must adjust to individual situations and make their selection accordingly. Of course older children also enjoy being carried in arms and sung to like this before being put to bed.

Sandman (d, e)

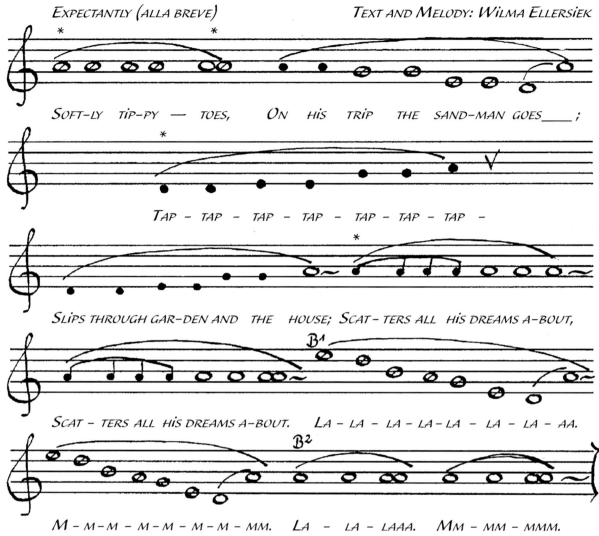

EXPECTANTLY (ALLA BREVE)   TEXT AND MELODY: WILMA ELLERSIEK

Soft-ly tip-py — toes,   On his trip the sand-man goes___ ;

Tap - tap - tap - tap - tap - tap - tap -

Slips through gar-den and the   house; Scat-ters all his dreams a-bout,

Scat - ters all his dreams a-bout.   La - la - la - la - la - la - la - aa.

M - m - m - m - m - m - m - mm.   La - la - laaa.   Mm - mm - mmm.

NOTATION: ⊘ ≈ ONE SLOW PULSATION (BASIC UNIT) / ●● ≈ ⊘ FOR A SLOW PULSATION TWO NOTES IN A MIDDLE TEMPO / ♪♪♪♪ ≈ ⊘ FOR ONE SLOW PULSATION FOUR NOTES IN A FAST TEMPO / O ≈ ⊘⊘ / ∞ ≈ ⊘⊘⊘⊘ / V ≈ ● PAUSE FOR THE DURATION OF A HALF SLOW PULSATION / ⌢ ≈ SLUR / ～ ≈ SOUND OUT LONGER / ⌒ ONE BREATH

TEXT:

1   Softly tippy-toes,

TOUCH:

1   Move hands (palms for-
    ward) down in a light
    soothing, calming gesture.

The child lies in bed or in
her lap as Mother sings this
song. While singing, she can
make some appropriate gestures, e.g. the sandman can
tap - tap on the bed cover.
Then her hands will let the
dreams float down from above
(finger movements).

For Part B of the song, sim-

90

2   On his trip the sandman
                              goes;

3   Tap – tap – tap – tap –
             tap – tap – tap –

4   Slips through garden

5   and the house;

6   Scatters all his dreams
                    about,
   Scatters all his dreams
                    about.

2   Lift hands to show a tassel cap on your head. Make a small bow to the front, then back. Sing the word "goes" a little more slowly.

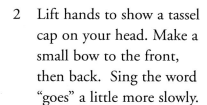

3   Tap with pointertips on thighs and move forward (to knee) in speech rhythm, taking turns right and left.

4   With palms together move hands forward with a little spring. Spread hands apart, one next to the other (palms down) to show a garden.

5   Move hands together above head. Fingertips touch to show a "roof." Hold a moment.

6   Take hands down, (palms down) moving them outward horizontally while wiggling fingers lightly and loosely, slowly and with care. Move hands up to shoulder height as in 5.

ple instruments instead of the voice can be use.

CYMBALS

For B1: with lifted forearms hold cymbals next to each other at chest height and after a gentle stroke make the following movement:

When the sound has completely died down, repeat stroke and gesture.

For B2 use initial posture as above, strike even more softly and make arc only shoulder high, but further forward toward the middle.

Repeat three times. Every new stroke is softer and leads into absolute silence. After the last "touch" of the cymbals lift them only lightly, no more arc and let the sound die out completely.

For parts B1 and B2 one can also use metal sound tubes, glockenspiel, or a triangle. At * in the music strike the triangle: on the tone A above, on the tone D below. At the text word "scatters," move the rod

7 *silent movement*

8 La — la — la — la — la
— la — la — aa.
M – m – m – m – m –
m – m – mm

9 La — la — laaa. —
Mm – mm – mmm.

10 *silent movement*

7 Lift both hands together above head.

8 At the sounds "la - la," etc., lower hands to stomach height with light steady finger movements. At the sound "M - m" etc. move hands upward and inward in a small arc while holding fingers still. Let it die away. Repeat 7 and 8.

9 Move hands outward in two arcs with only a few finger movements. At "laaa" move hands in a small arc inward and lower without finger movement. Hold a moment. Repeat for "Mm - mm" etc.

10 Let hands sink on thighs. To show the dreams floating down, the hand gestures must be very "airy."

quickly in the top triangle corner. At the text word "dreams," let the sound die down.

Tired is My Baby (b, c)

Gently lulling to sleep

Text and Melody: Wilma Ellersiek

Tir – ed   is   my   ba – by   dear, — Slips   be – tween the   cov – ers here;

In   her   bed feels safe – ly guard – ed,   Deep – ly   sleeps till morn – ing's start – ed.

Soo – soo – soo – soo!   Eyes   are   clos – ing   too_____.

Soo – oo – soo – oo – soo – oo – soo!   Soo – soo – soo!

Soo – oo – soo – oo – soo – oo – soo!   Soo – soo – soo!

Ending: for voice or instruments

NOTATION: ● ≈ ONE PULSATION (BASIC UNIT) / ∅ ≈ ●● / ○ ≈ ●●●●
⌒ ≈ SLUR / ∼ ≈ SOUND OUT LONGER / ⌣ ≈ DYING OUT AT THE SAME TIME
GROWING SLOWER AND SOFTER / ⌒ ≈ ONE BREATH / ↶ ↷ ≈ ROCKING

All the Dear Stars (a, e)

CHEERFUL-QUIETLY SWINGING

TEXT AND MELODY: WILMA ELLERSIEK

1) ALL THE DEAR STARS IN THE HEAV - ENS FREE,
2) ALL THE DEAR STARS_____ THEIR WATCH DO KEEP,
3) LA LA LA LA LA LA LA LA LA

1) DOWN THEY ARE GAZ - ING ON LAND AND SEA.
2) WHILE I AM ROCK - ING BA - BY TO SLEEP,
3) LA LA LA LA LA LA LA LA LA

1) TWIN-KLING IN DARK - NESS WITH SHIM - MER - ING RAY,
2) SHIN-ING AND BLINK-ING WITH SIL - VER - Y LIGHT,
3) MM MM MM MM MM MM MM MM MM MM

1) WHO CAN, DEAR STARS, WHO YOUR NUM-BERS CAN SAY?
2) WAVE FROM A - BOVE IN THE HEAV-ENS: "GOOD NIGHT!"
3) MM MM MM MM MM MM MM MM MM MM

1) ALL THE DEAR STARS IN THE HEAV - ENS FREE,
2) ALL THE DEAR STARS_____ THEIR WATCH DO KEEP,
3) LA LA LA LA LA LA LA LA LA

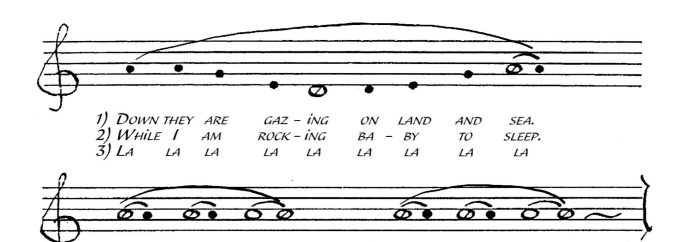

1) DOWN THEY ARE GAZ – ING ON LAND AND SEA.
2) WHILE I AM ROCK – ING BA – BY TO SLEEP.
3) LA LA LA LA LA LA LA LA LA

MM MM MMM – MM MM MMM – !

NOTATION: ● ≈ ONE PULSATION (BASIC UNIT) | Ø ≈ ●● | ⌒ ● ≈ ●●● | ⌒⌒ ≈
●●●●●● | ~ ≈ SOUND OUT LONGER | ⌒ ≈ ONE BREATH

TEXT:

1   All the dear stars in the
           heavens free,

TOUCH:

1   Hands with fingers spread
    wide (stars) are lifted slant-
    ingly above head. At
    "heavens" hold them still.

In the winter when it darkens early so that at bedtime the stars are already shining in the sky, Mother can stand by the window with her child on her arm, sing this song and accompany it with a few appropriate gestures with her free hand. The movements should be subtle, leaving the child free to experience being protected not only by humans but also by heavenly beings, who envelop and carry him. It is important that he can snuggle up to his mother at the same time in order to also experience bodily protection.

The song is also very suitable for singing in groups. Depending on the situation, it can be accompanied with hand gestures.

2   Down they are gazing on
      land and sea.

2   Slanting forward move
    hands down a little, hold-
    ing them still again at "on
    land and sea."

3   Twinkling in darkness with
     x right   x left
           shimmering ray,
             x   x
Who can, dear stars,
    x   x

3   In given speech rhythm "x," move hands forward, right and left in turn, spreading fingers more strongly. Give a little "push" at the end of the movement to show the twinkling of the stars.

4   who your numbers can
                   say?

4   Turn your hands from palms forward to palms up, like two bowls, or like a question. Look up.

5   All the dear stars in the
              heavens free,

5   Move hands up in an arc to same position as in 1.

6	Down they are gazing on land and sea.	6	As in 2.
7	All the dear stars	7	As in 1.
8	their watch do keep	8	Move hands down and touch palm to palm.
9	While I am rocking baby to sleep,	9	Rest left cheek on hands, with this gesture lightly rock to and fro.

9 While I am rocking baby
        to sleep,

9 Rest left cheek on hands,
   with this gesture lightly
   rock to and fro.

10 Shining and blinking with
        x   x
            silvery light,
            x   x

10 As above in 3 at head
    height.

11 <u>Wave</u> from <u>above</u> in the
        <u>heavens:</u> "Good night!"

11 In given rhythm — — —,
    wave with both hands at
    the same time. After the
    last wave move hands for-
    ward and down, a protect-
    ing gesture.

12 All the dear stars
13 their watch do keep
14 while I am rocking baby to
        sleep.
15 mm-mm-mmmm
        mm-mm-mmmm
16 silent

12 As in 7.
13 As in 8.
14 As in 9.

15 Keep same gesture and
    rock lightly.
16 Sit awhile quietly, then
    dissolve gesture.

All to Rest Must Go (e)

Swinging quietly

Text and Melody: Wilma Ellersiek

So-so-so, all to rest must go; Soo-soo-soo, ba-by, sleep now, too.

In their co-zy nest bird-ies take their rest.

So-so-so, all to rest must go; Soo-soo-soo, ba-by, sleep now, too.

In the barn the sheep dream in slum-ber deep.

So-so-so, all to rest must go; Soo-soo-soo, ba-by, sleep now, too.

In the heav-ens far twin-kle man-y stars.

So-so-so, all to rest must go; soo-soo-soo, ba-by, sleep now, too.

So - so - so — soo - soo - soooo ! —

<u>NOTATION:</u> ● ≈ ONE PULSATION (BASIC UNIT) / ♩♩ ≈ ● FOR ONE PULSATION TWO NOTES IN FAST TEMPO / ⊘ ≈ ● ● / ⊘ ≈ ● ● ● ● / ~ ≈ SOUND OUT LONGER / ⌒ ≈ ONE BREATH / ↜ ↝ ≈ ROCKING

TEXT:

1 So — so — so, all to rest must go; Soo — soo — soo, baby, sleep now, too.

2 In their cozy nest birdies take their rest.

3 So — so — so,...;
Soo — soo — soo...(etc).

4 In the barn the sheep dream in slumber deep.

TOUCH:

1 Cross lower arms and rock an imaginary child, or a real child (or doll), in your lap.

2 Form a nest (bowl) with your hands in front of you. Rock to and fro.

3 As in 1.

4 Move arms up. Above the head, with both hands, form the roof of the "barn."

PRONUNCIATION:

So-so-so rhymes with "go."
Soo-soo-soo rhymes with "too."

5   So — so — so,...;
     Soo — soo — soo,....(etc)

5   As in 1 and 3.

6   In the heavens far twinkle many stars.

6   Lift hands (palms forward) pointing up. Lower hands to head height and at "twinkle," stretch fingers toward front. Move back with rolled fingers and repeat movement to front as "stars" (the stars shine and glitter).

7   So — so — so,...;
     Soo — soo — soo... (etc)

7   As 1, 3 and 5.

8   Soo — soo — soo! —

8   Movement and singing slowly die away.

Humming to Sleep (c)

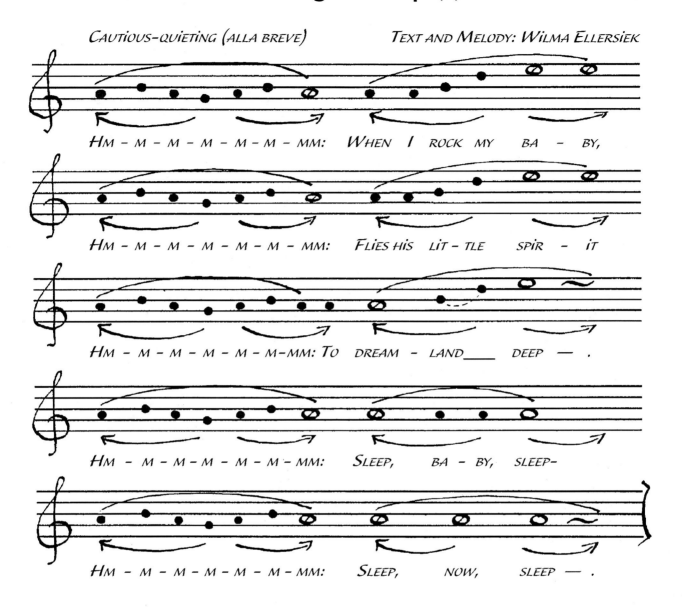

Cautious-quieting (alla breve)

Text and Melody: Wilma Ellersiek

Hm - m - m - m - m - m - mm: When I rock my ba - by,

Hm - m - m - m - m - m - mm: Flies his lit - tle spir - it

Hm - m - m - m - m - m - mm: To dream - land___ deep — .

Hm - m - m - m - m - m - mm: Sleep, ba - by, sleep-

Hm - m - m - m - m - m - mm: Sleep, now, sleep — .

NOTATION: ⊘ ≈ ONE SLOW PULSATION (BASIC UNIT) | ● ● ≈ ⊘ FOR A SLOW PULSATION TWO NOTES IN MEDIUM TEMPO | O ≈ ⊘⊘ | ~ ≈ SOUND OUT LONGER ⌒ ≈ ONE BREATH | ↶ ↷ ≈ ROCKING

With this song it is especially lovely to play along with the Choroi harp. The humming can then be played on the harp. Children love to be rocked in your lap at the same time, and also like it when you sit by their bed and sing and play.

Striking the strings is not a plucking from above but rather a stroking across the strings with your finger, to achieve a milder tone.

SONGS FOR ADULTS

Songs in the Mood of the Fifth (*Quint*) with Central Tone A for Adults

The following songs have been added here to give adults an opportunity to acquaint themselves at their own level with the tonal space of the fifth interval with central tone A without major and minor modes, swinging in the tonal space of the ninth interval.[1] Thus the adult can hear and live into the tonal space, so that she will be able to sing correctly, and later create songs herself for the children in the first seven years of life and beyond. Songs in the mood of the fifth have a healing quality for people who are ill. They liberate us from emotional stress and strengthen the life forces.

Always sing the songs at the pitch or tone indicated. However, beat and tone duration may be freely varied; the songs can be sung according to the rhythm of speech.

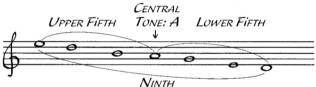

*Pentatonic mood of the fifth
(original ancient Greek form) with central tone A*

[1] See "Mood of the Fifth," p. 78

The Star

Bright-flowing and slow   TEXT AND MELODY: WILMA ELLERSIEK

BE-TWEEN BIR-CHES AND HEM-LOCK TREES STANDS IN HEAV-EN FAR A STAR, A___ STAR. WITH ITS BLUE AND SIL-VER___ SHINE BEAM-ING IN THIS ROOM OF_ MINE. TWIN-KLES, TWIN-KLES SO KIND-LY AS___ I SLEEP, FILLS MY HEART WITH QUI-ET, QUI-ET DEEP. BE-TWEEN BIRCH-ES AND HEM-LOCK TREES BEAMS FROM HEAV-EN_ FAR MY STAR! MY STAR! —

When a Mother Her Baby is Rocking

Swinging quietly   Text: Gottfried Wolters/Melody: Wilma Ellersiek

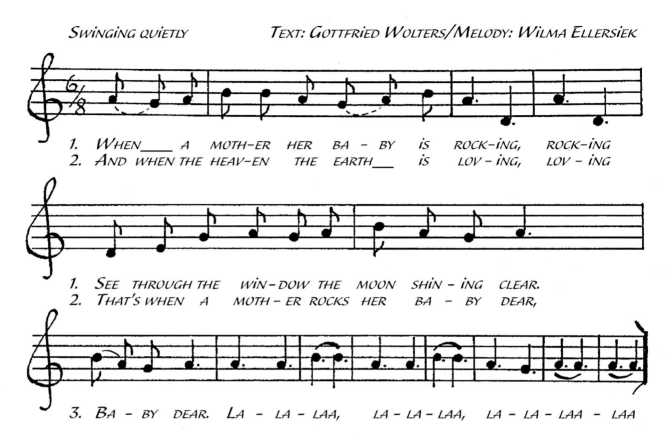

1. When____ a moth-er her ba - by is rock-ing, rock-ing
2. And when the heav-en the earth____ is lov - ing, lov - ing

1. See through the win-dow the moon shin - ing clear.
2. That's when a moth - er rocks her ba - by dear,

3. Ba - by dear. La - la - laa, la - la - laa, la - la - laa - laa

Let Your Destiny Bide

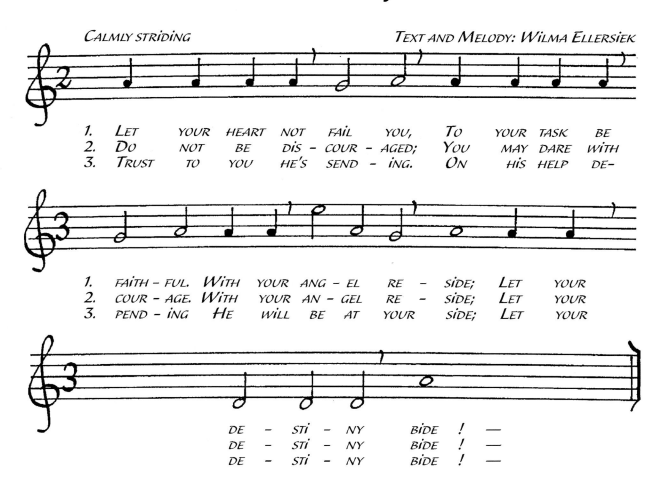

Calmly striding

Text and Melody: Wilma Ellersiek

1. LET YOUR HEART NOT FAIL YOU, To YOUR TASK BE
2. Do NOT BE DIS - COUR - AGED; You MAY DARE WITH
3. TRUST TO YOU HE'S SEND - ING. ON HIS HELP DE-

1. FAITH - FUL. WITH YOUR ANG - EL RE - SIDE; LET YOUR
2. COUR - AGE. WITH YOUR AN - GEL RE - SIDE; LET YOUR
3. PEND - ING HE WILL BE AT YOUR SIDE; LET YOUR

1. DE - STI - NY BIDE ! —
2. DE - STI - NY BIDE ! —
3. DE - STI - NY BIDE ! —

Alternating 2/2 and 3/2 time signature. As an ending, "let your destiny bide" may be repeated.

WILMA ELLERSIEK: A LIFE FOR RHYTHM

In a small village in Schleswig-Holstein, directly on the coastline of the Baltic Sea, on June 15, 1921, Wilma Ellersiek first saw the light of the world. With the rhythm of the waves, the murmur of the wind, and with dogs, cats, chickens, ducks and a horse as playmates, she lived a childhood bound up with nature. Her friends were, as she says, flowers, trees, sand and stars. But above all, rhythm, encountered at the seaside in many-layered forms, would stay with Wilma Ellersiek throughout her life. Looking back, she perceives her childhood as an almost heavenly life in the rhythm of nature. In her parents' home she was encouraged to pursue music, but also language and literature. Nature on one hand and culture on the other were an ideal, marvelous and edifying atmosphere for developing one's humanity.

In 1927 the Ellersiek family moved to Westphalia. Again little Wilma had the luck of living next-door to a farm; so the dear creatures remained her friends as before. New, however, was the impression of grain fields waving in the breeze, another rhythmic wave movement. Now came early meetings with other children, first in kindergarten and soon also in school. Their time together was filled with singing, dancing and recitation; indeed, looking back she sees her entire childhood and youth as suffused with music and rhythm a sound basis for her later activity.

Wilma Ellersiek completed her schooldays with the *Abitur* examination and in 1941 she began to study in Leipzig, beginning in the major areas of school music, German philology and history of art. Serious sickness forced her to interrupt her study. This was followed by the confusion of wartime, near the end of which, in 1945, her family was forced to flee from Eastern Europe. In Essen, Wilma Ellersiek resumed her study at the Volkwang School, albeit changing her major field. Her new field of study was rhythmic-musical education, continued in Stuttgart at the State Academy for Music and Performing Arts. There she became a student of Elfriede Feudel, herself a master student of the founder of "Eurhythmics," Émile Jaques-Dalcroze.[1] In addition to studying eurhythmics, Wilma Ellersiek also entered the study of speech education and completed both fields in 1957 with the state examination. Eurhythmics then became her life's content. She remained at the Stuttgart Music Academy as an assistant in the three departments: Eurhythmics, Theater and Spoken Word. After her time as assistant, she was offered a lecturing position, and later a professorship. In addition to her work at the Academy, she worked as stage director in opera and drama in Stuttgart, Vienna and London, among other places.

Again a serious sickness caused a decisive change in vocation, and again it was rhythm that fascinated her. Wilma Ellersiek now turned to research on the specific effects of rhythm and movement, language and music on the small child. Her work on this theme provoked attention, and in 1968 she received a research commission for it from the State of Baden-Württemberg. Out of this impulse the first "gesture-games" for the pre-school child were born. Out of these little gesture-games, step-by-step, with enviable intuition, and also with enormous exactitude and care, she developed great, connected play-units in rhyme, interwoven with rhythm and music. In the beginning she called her courses "School for Parents," for her idea was to teach children together with mothers or fathers. In the late 1960's, the Stuttgart Music Academy established for Wilma Ellersiek, within the Eurhythmics Department, the specialty "Eurhythmics for the Preschool Age." During this time, a meeting took place with the "matriarch" of the Waldorf kindergartens, Klara Hattermann, with whom she maintains an intimate friendship to this day. Klara Hattermann has viewed the new games with interest, has accompanied Wilma Ellersiek through many difficulties and has encouraged again and again her continued activity. Along with several of Wilma Ellersiek's students from Stuttgart, Klara Hattermann has carried the games into the world through workshops. After 25 years of intensive teaching activity, Wilma Ellersiek retired, leaving the Academy in 1983. Lifted out of her teaching responsibilities, she became more creative than ever. Many of the games were developed at this time, among which are all the caresses and many lullabies. Additionally, during this time, a circle of interested friends came together in Hannover around Klara Hattermann to work intensively with the games of Wilma Ellersiek and see to their propagation in a form as true as possible to the intention of their author.

The games of Wilma Ellersiek come from her listening to Nature; in a way true to their origin she has succeeded in artistically molding speech, rhythm and the corresponding gestures to bring the wind, flowers, beasts, sun, moon and stars into the child's presence through little musical tales. In this way through the swinging, healing, natural rhythms of the games, she offers something to today's children from her own nature-filled childhood.

Ingrid Weidenfeld

[1] Dalcroze's Eurhythmics: not to be confused with the art of movement developed by Rudolf Steiner, called "Eurythmy."

Addresses

Waldorf Early Childhood Association of North America,
(WECAN)
285 Hungry Hollow Rd.
Spring Valley, NY 10977
Tel. (845) 352-1690
e-mail: info@waldorfearlychildhood.org

International Association of Waldorf Kindergartens
Heubergstr. 18
D-70188 Stuttgart, Germany
Tel. (07 11) 925 740
Internet: www.waldorfkindergarten.org
E-Mail: inter.waldorf@t-online.de

Vereinigung für die authentische Weitergabe der Spiele von W. Ellersiek
Irmela Möller
Wiehbeg str. 37
30519 Hannover
E-Mail: s.weidenfeld@t-online.de

Lyn and Kundry Willwerth
2760 Webb Rd.
Cortland, NY 13045
Tel. (607) 756-2782
E-Mail: frauwillwerth@hotmail.com

Choroi Instruments
available at:
Rudolf Steiner College Bookstore
9200 Fair Oaks Blvd.
Fair Oaks, CA 95628
Tel. (916) 961-8729

Quintenlieder: Music for Young Children in the Mood of the Fifth
by Julius Knierim
Rudolf Steiner College Press, 1994
available through Rudolf Steiner College Bookstore
Tel. (916) 961-8729

Learning CDs for *Giving Love - Bringing Joy* and
Gesture Games for Spring and Summer, Autumn and Winter
available at:
Hillside Kindergarten
2760 Webb Rd.
Cortland, NY 13045
Tel. (607) 756-2782
E-Mail: frauwillwerth@hotmail.com

Gesture Games for Spring and Summer

By Wilma Ellersiek
Edited and translated by Kundry and Lyn Willwerth
Illustrations by Friederike Loegters
138 pages with Spiral binding.
Publisher: WECAN

The seasons spring and summer have inspired poets and musicians alike to celebrate the renewal of spring and its fulfillment.

We all know that young children show a spontaneous interest in any little ant or pebble that needs to be touched and explored. In sharing the experiences of the innumerable small wonders of nature with our children we can awaken in them feelings of love, concern and responsibility for the life of our planet.

These songs, hand gestures and movement games for the seasons of spring and summer by Wilma Ellersiek lead our children to joyful participation and understanding of nature around them.